The Cultural Revolution
at Peking University

The Cultural Revolution
at Peking University

by Victor Nee
with Don Layman

New York and London

Copyright © 1969 by Victor Nee
All Rights Reserved

Library of Congress Catalog Card Number: 77-81790

First Printing

Published by Monthly Review Press
116 West 14th Street, New York, N.Y. 10011
33/37 Moreland Street, London, E.C. 1

Manufactured in the United States of America

To rebellious parents, teachers,
and students everywhere

Note

This essay began as a Master's thesis written by Victor Nee at Harvard University for Professor Ezra Vogel. Don Layman then brought forward important additional documents, and considerably revised and expanded our treatment of the period since 1964.

We want to thank Bill Hinton, whose book *Fanshen* has greatly inspired us, as well as Professors John Israel, Carl Riskin, and Franz Schurmann for their helpful criticism of the original paper. The encouragement and criticism of our friends Tom Engelhardt, Elizabeth Graf, Deirdre and Neale Hunter, Virginia Layman, and Jim Peck have been invaluable to us in the final stages. Special thanks to Susan Lowes of Monthly Review for generous editorial care. Finally, the thoughts in these pages belong mainly to the students and teachers of Peking University, and we hope they will send us their additions and corrections.

We should add that we have used the Wade-Giles system in romanizing Chinese characters.

—V.N.
—D.L.L.

Contents

1

The Hundred Flowers and the Educational Revolution of 1958

Peking University, familiarly called Peita in China, was founded as the Imperial University in 1898. It has been the country's most celebrated modern institution of higher learning, as well as its oldest. By the early 1960's Peita had about 10,000 students in its eighteen faculties.

Like universities elsewhere, it has never existed in a social vacuum. In 1918 Mao Tse-tung worked there as a library assistant under Li Ta-chao, the head librarian and professor of political economy who is credited with being the academic figure who introduced Marxist ideas to China. The following year, when the Paris Peace Conference sought to award Japan the former German sphere of influence in China, Li Ta-chao strongly opposed the treaty, and Peita students took a leading role in the May 4th Movement of protest which soon spread over much of the country. News of the movement in Peking inspired Mao, who had returned to his native Hunan, to help organize a student union and a strike in Ch'angsha. Participation in the strikes and the boycotting of Japanese goods, although still limited to a fairly narrow stratum of urban intellectuals, workers, and patriotic merchants, nevertheless compelled the Peking government to dismiss pro-Japanese diplomats and to refuse to sign the Versailles Treaty. In December 1935, Peking students led the demonstrations against Kuomintang capitulation to Japanese encroachment. These demonstrations were violently suppressed, and a number of Peita students subsequently left the city to join the Red Army in the revolutionary base areas of Yenan.

Despite this patriotic and revolutionary tradition among the students, Peking University was also a bastion of conservative and reactionary forces, especially its administration. The influence of privileged foreigners was reflected in many ways, including the school's adoption of the costly English tutorial system. Though many students and instructors were liberal democrats, and even intellectual radicals, they naturally came for the most part from wealthy families. When the new revolutionary government was established in Peking in 1949, much of the old staff remained; and while teachers and administrators tended to give the Communist Party credit for leading a national "self-strengthening" movement, few were Party members, and fewer still had known the life of revolutionary combat in North China's mud, side by side with members of China's worker and peasant majority.

In 1952, in the course of a major reorganization of Peking's universities and institutes, Peita was moved from the city proper to the western suburbs, where it occupied the premises of Yenching University, which was disbanded. Memories of Leighton Stuart, a missionary who had become Yenching's president in 1919 and who had been Ambassador to the Kuomintang regime from 1946 to 1949, were still fresh.[1]

With the inauguration of the first Five Year Plan in 1953, the Chinese higher-education system, inadequate to the needs of rapid industrialization, underwent drastic structural transformation. The old Kuomintang system, which had been modeled largely on Anglo-American institutions, now began to be reshaped to Soviet patterns. Soviet teaching plans, curricula, and textbooks were translated without modification so that

---

1. These remarks draw on an article entitled "How It All Started in Peking University" (hereafter cited as "How It All Started") by A. Jackson-Thomas, K. Janaka, and A. Manheim, in *Eastern Horizon* (Hong Kong), Vol. VI, No. 5 (May 1967), p. 21, and on Jerome Ch'en, *Mao and the Chinese Revolution* (New York: Oxford University Press, 1965), p. 62. The authors of "How It All Started" live in Peking.

China could draw on "the advanced experience of the Soviet Union in . . . teaching methods and curricula."[2]

Because the course content had to be highly technical and specialized in order to train large numbers of scientists, engineers, and technicians as rapidly as possible, the tendency was to recruit from among the best-educated urban secondary-school students. In most instances these were students from bourgeois and landlord families. Despite efforts to reverse this trend, even by 1955 only about 28 percent of the students were from worker and peasant families.[3]

In the classroom, emphasis was placed on scientific professionalism and technical expertise. Marxist political re-education and manual labor were relegated to a secondary position despite the efforts of many Party cadres to stress them. Chinese education began more and more to resemble its contemporary Soviet model.

But Soviet education was not what it had been in the decade following the October Revolution. The climate of lively experimentation, anti-authoritarianism, and involvement in the broader society which had then prevailed in Soviet schools had been the envy of progressive educators around the world. In the early years of the first Soviet Five Year Plan, introduced in 1928, it was common for schools to assist a factory directly in fulfilling its part in the Plan; school workshops were popular and polytechnical education was stressed. But in 1931, when it appeared that students were receiving insufficient conventional knowledge, an extreme reversal of educational policy took place. Central Committee decrees insisted that basic subjects be taught separately, in the traditional manner, "using

---

2. New China News Agency (hereafter cited as NCNA), November 24, 1952.

3. *Peking Review*, No. 12, 1958, cited by Stewart Fraser in *Chinese Communist Education: Records of the First Decade* (Nashville, Tenn.: Vanderbilt University Press, 1965), p. 16. According to an interview with Hu Cha, director of a department in the Ministry of Higher Education, the percentage of university-level students of working-class or peasant origin was 20.46 in 1952, 36.42 in 1958, 42.34 in 1962, and 49.65 in 1965. See K. S. Karol, *China: The Other Communism*, 2nd ed. (New York: Hill & Wang, 1968), p. 300.

the recitation method, with individual student responsibility for mastering the material."

The idea that the factory, trade-union, or village Soviet could partially replace certain school functions was thoroughly repudiated. The accent was on formal studies, involving primarily book learning. Grades and examinations were emphasized as they had not been since Tsarist times, with individual competition for high grades encouraged. The teacher was restored to a position of dignity and authority in the classroom and pupils were required to show respect and deference for the teacher. The activities of pupils' organizations were greatly curtailed and they were made completely subservient to the school authorities.[4]

From the mid-1930's on, Soviet education in the social sciences began to emphasize Russian nationalism, playing down the historical-materialist analysis of broad social currents and exalting such figures as Peter the Great.

As the revolutionary aspects of the Soviet system were supplanted by the drive for stability and conformity, one by one the principles upon which Soviet education had originally been built were discarded and replaced. Following the demise of such things as the complex-method and active learning through doing came the end of polytechnical education, the most unique aspect of Marxist educational theory.[5]

Such changes in Soviet society were reflected in the ascendancy within the Soviet Communist Party (CPSU) of a technocratic elite which had taken the place of the large number of working-class Party members murdered in the 1930's along with so many of Lenin's better known intellectual associates. In 1930 workers made up 65.3 percent of the CPSU and "intelligentsia and other employees" made up 14.5 percent. By 1956, workers made up only 32 percent, while "intellectuals and other employees" held an absolute majority with 50.9 percent.[6]

4. Ruth Widmayer, "A Historical Survey of Soviet Education," in *Soviet Society: A Book of Readings,* ed. Alex Inkeles and Kent Geiger (Boston: Houghton Mifflin, 1961), p. 435.
5. *Ibid.,* pp. 435-436.
6. Data cited by Boris Meissner, "The Power Elite and Intelligentsia in Soviet Society," in *The Soviet Union: A Half-Century of Communism,* ed. Kurt London (Baltimore: John Hopkins University Press, 1968), pp. 158, 168.

Was China to take the same path?

By 1956, China had undergone three years of rapid economic growth under the Soviet-style first Five Year Plan. Political unity had been established, a Korean War armistice achieved, the country's socialist economy appeared basically consolidated, and agricultural collectivization had proceeded rapidly and effectively, with active leadership in the hands of poor and lower-middle peasants. At this time, the Party's leadership decided to reassess its policy toward intellectuals and students. As had happened in the Soviet Union, rapid industrialization was demanding increased reliance on the technical expertise of the intelligentsia, and the demand for experts still greatly exceeded the available supply.

In a speech delivered to the Central Committee in January 1956, Premier Chou En-lai called for the improvement of material conditions for intellectuals by raising university salaries, improved research conditions, and reduced political and administrative assignments.[7] In May of the same year, Mao Tse-tung and Lu Ting-yi called on students and intellectuals to "Let a hundred flowers bloom, a hundred schools of thought contend." In announcing a general relaxation of political supervision, Lu promised the intelligentsia "freedom of independent thinking, of debate, of creative work; freedom to criticize and freedom to express, maintain, and reserve one's opinions on questions of art, literature or scientific research."[8]

Though Mao, Chou, and Lu called for a new policy toward the intelligentsia, many Party cadres, feeling their positions threatened, were slow in relaxing political control. In February 1957, impatient with the slow response of middle- and lower-level Party members, Mao announced a campaign against the "Three Evils" within the Party: bureaucratism, sectarianism, and subjectivism. Mao appears to have placed the blame for

7. Chou En-lai, "On the Question of Intellectuals," in Robert R. Bowie and John K. Fairbank, *Communist China, 1955-59* (Cambridge, Mass.: Harvard University Press, 1962), pp. 129-130.
8. Lu Ting-yi, "Let a Hundred Flowers Blossom, a Hundred Schools of Thought Contend!" (May 26, 1956) in Bowie and Fairbank, p. 153.

the 1956 Hungarian uprising largely on the Hungarian Party's isolation from the masses and on its rigid control of the intellectuals.[9] In calling for a rectification campaign, Mao hoped to check similar trends which had developed within the Chinese Communist Party, and students and other intellectuals were urged to participate.

Though students at first were reluctant to respond to the call for "blooming and contending," on May 19, 1957, a group at Peking University put up the first *tatzupao* ("big-character" wall posters) attacking the Party's treatment of the intellectuals. News of the activity at Peita quickly spread to the other major universities. Soon a student movement sprang up which in varying degrees criticized almost every aspect of the Party's rule in China.[10]

For the most part, students approved of the ideals of the Party; their criticism was that the Party did not live up to its own proclaimed ideals. Peita students criticized excesses and abuses of power by Party cadres during the *Su-fan* movement in 1955, a movement against counter-revolutionaries and "rascals."[11] Some students criticized the way of life of the various Party members who had acquired special privileges and who "used the fruits of socialism as a ladder to climb to higher positions." They criticized cadres who had developed arrogant and haughty attitudes toward the people and denounced their bureaucratic work-style, arguing that they had become new "mandarins." In short, the main thrust of the students' criticism was directed against the Party bureaucracy, which many felt had been transformed from a revolutionary organization into an elite club. In a debate held at Peita on May 23, Lin Hsi-ling, a People's University student argued:

During the tempest of the revolution, Party members stayed

---

9. See Mao's "On the Correct Handling of Contradictions Among the People" (February 27, 1957).
10. Rene Goldman, "The Rectification Campaign at Peking University: May-June 1957," in Roderick MacFarquhar's *China Under Mao: Politics Takes Command* (Cambridge, Mass.: MIT Press, 1966), p. 258. Goldman was a student at Peita during this period.
11. *Ibid.*, p. 260.

together with the people; but after the victory of the revolution, they climbed into the ruling position. . . . The ruler and the ruled are in different positions; they look at problems from different angles and their interests are not the same. . . . Genuine socialism should be very democratic . . . we must struggle for genuine socialism. Socialism belongs to the people, not only to the Party members. All the people should be allowed to air their views to their hearts' content. The present "blooming and contending" is confined to the upper strata only. This won't do . . . Let the broad masses discuss and air their opinions and then synthesize these opinions. This is the ideal way.[12]

But what had caused the growth of this inequality between Party members and the broad masses? A Peita student wrote that "external factors . . . play an important part in the growth of the Three Evils in Communist China. To direct our attention to external factors in order to study the roots of the Three Evils in the Soviet Union is . . . essential."[13]

Lin Hsi-ling focused her criticism on "the personnel system, the system of ranks, the enlargement of the security system," which she associated with Soviet practices under Stalin. The personnel system allotted special privileges to Party members, and the ranking system stratified students, teachers, and Party members in a rigid hierarchy.[14] Lin saw foreign influence in the development of the Three Evils, and attacked the "wild copying of the Soviet Union. . . . The compradors toadied to foreigners and worshiped America; now our learning from the Soviet Union is just like that." Other Peita students criticized other aspects of the Soviet educational model, including both institutional structure and course content. They disliked the dogmatic application of Soviet "Marxist" thought and felt that some Soviet textbooks were chauvinistic and boring.

Though most Peita students criticized the Party from the

---

12. Quoted in Dennis Doolin, *Communist China: The Politics of Student Opposition* (Palo Alto: Stanford University Press, 1964), pp. 23-29.
13. *Ibid.,* p. 56.
14. For a liberal sociologist's view of these developments, see Ezra Vogel's article "From Revolutionary to Semi-Bureaucrat, The 'Regularisation' of Cadres," *China Quarterly,* No. 29 (January-March 1967), pp. 36-40.

standpoint of egalitarian ideals, they had not come to terms with their own intellectual elitism. The very same students who had criticized Party elitism opposed the work-study program which called on intellectuals to combine manual labor with mental labor; Lin Hsi-ling alleged that "the masses don't necessarily want them [the intellectuals] to come to work; they want them to come and run things as they should be run."[15] Some students and teachers demanded that Party committees either be withdrawn from educational institutions or limited in power— in order to "let the professors run the universities."[16]

In China, where intellectuals historically have had a high degree of access to political power, the student criticism of the Party can be interpreted as a bid to wrest political power from the hands of poorly educated Party cadres, many of whom had been workers and peasants. Political power would not be transferred to the masses under such a dispensation; rather, it would be returned to its "rightful holder," the lettered elite. Small wonder that middle- and lower-level cadres and even many high-ranking Party officials so strongly opposed Mao's policy of "blooming and contending."[17]

Although student criticism was primarily reformist, a few students did advocate the overthrow of Communist Party rule. The students who attacked the Communist Party from the political Right argued that "Marxism is out of date. . . . Instead we must learn from the democracy and freedom of the capitalist countries, and turn to a new interpretation of capitalism."[18] Some who called for the restoration of capitalism wrote posters containing such slogans as "Exterminate the Com-

15. Doolin, *op. cit.*, p. 34.
16. *Ibid.*, p. 66.
17. According to Lin Hsi-ling, "The 'blooming and contending' suggested by the Party Central Committee has encountered much resistance. The Chairman said that more than ninety percent of the high-ranking cadres were opposed to the idea."—Doolin, *op. cit.*, p. 33. Also see Merle Goldman's discussion of the Hundred Flowers Campaign in his *Literary Dissent in Communist China* (Cambridge, Mass.: Harvard University Press, 1967), pp. 180-182.
18. Roderick MacFarquhar, *The Hundred Flowers Campaign and the Chinese Intellectuals* (New York: Frederick Praeger, 1960), p. 136.

munist bandits," "The Party members are secret agents and they are worse than the Japanese agents during the occupation period," and "What a dull thing is this socialism."[19]

In their criticism of the larger society they also attacked major Party projects. A few students at Kwangsi Normal College, for example, not only opposed the Party's favoring the admission of students from peasant and worker families, but also sharply criticized its agricultural collectivization program. These students condemned collectivization as a "repressive measure against the peasants who were forced to submit, or they would have no land to till." Their feeling was that the "society was in a mess and another revolution was necessary."[20]

Mao Tse-tung clearly agreed with the students who had criticized Party cadres as being guilty of the Three Evils (bureaucratism, sectarianism, and subjectivism): eliciting such criticism had been the aim of the rectification campaign. But as a Marxist he opposed the ideas of those students with an elitist mentality, those who demanded special privileges, and those who advocated counter-revolution. He must have been acutely aware of the fact that almost 70 percent of the university students came from bourgeois and landlord families. Furthermore, he must have recognized that much of the opposition from the political Right was prompted by the attitudes of professors, who were mostly members of the former ruling classes.[21] A Marxist was bound to feel that the existing education system was undermining the revolution.

19. *Ibid.*, pp. 147-151.
20. *Ibid.*, p. 147.
21. "According to statistics relating to the 2,474 professors and assistant professors in forty-six institutions of higher education in China, the absolute majority of them came from landlord and bourgeois families and only a few individuals came from working-class families. More than 98 percent of them received their higher education in old China, which was soaked with the class spirit of the bourgeoisie. A very considerable proportion had also gone abroad to study in European and American capitalist countries. The absolute majority of them have passed middle age. This is to say that they have spent the greater part of their lives in the old society."—NCNA, January 19, 1959.

The fact that so many of the new "experts" had had only traditional liberal ideas to offer during the Hundred Flowers movement—ideas which at best seemed insufficient for comprehending Chinese reality and for correcting the abuses the students perceived—was probably what led Mao to a final disillusionment with the Soviet model for social change. Just as he had opposed the dogmatic application of the Bolshevik revolutionary experience to the Chinese situation after 1927, he once again called for the "creative application" of the principles of Marxism-Leninism to the practical needs of the Chinese revolution. His search for more relevant ideas crystallized in the program which became known as the "Great Leap Forward," itself largely inspired by the upsurge of large-scale water-resource control projects being undertaken by some of the new peasant cooperatives.

The Great Leap swiftly followed the campaign which was launched in June 1957 against Rightists and counter-revolutionaries, many of whom had revealed their "unreformed" ideas in the previous months of "blooming and contending." An integral part of the Leap was the Educational Revolution, whose purpose was to transform the school system from a "bourgeois haven" into a revolutionary environment. The new system was to be radically different from both the Anglo-American and the latter-day Soviet models, and was to educate a "new socialist man," who had both political consciousness and culture and who was capable of both mental and physical labor.

One of the most important aspects of the Educational Revolution was that it included a massive program to democratize enrollment policy. As already noted, the universities had previously recruited from among those most easily educable by traditional standards—the students of bourgeois, professional, and landlord backgrounds. In a country where peasants constituted over 80 percent of the population, the social composition of the universities in 1957 presented a very narrow base from which future leaders could be drawn. If the effects of this recruitment policy were allowed to accumulate, the social and political advantages enjoyed by the old ruling classes would be perpetuated. Experts might be trained, but what was to ensure that they would serve China's majority, the productive workers who provided the material conditions for the experts' education? Who was to benefit from economic growth and how was such growth to be sustained?

If China's large and rapidly growing population was to be a great resource rather than a burden, much depended on the extent to which popular enthusiasm was mobilized and scientific attitudes toward the problems of development spread to the remotest countryside. A technically expert elite divorced from industrial and agricultural labor would soon be tempted to exercise rigid control over the historically disadvantaged classes, while allying itself with congenial members of the old privileged classes and strata and adopting many of the latter's ways. Such a new privileged stratum would no doubt eventually go the way of the Kuomintang, but the greater political and technical sophistication of its members would probably make its overthrow a much more protracted and bloody affair.[22]

To help avert the need for such a second violent revolution, Mao and the Chinese Left in general agreed that it was essential to increase the enrollment of workers and peasants in higher education, and to assure their continued participation in the social life and political struggles of the milieu from which they came. The president of Tsinghua University announced the gist of the new policy:

The educational institution becomes not just a school, but at the same time a research institute, factory, designing institute, and building concern. An end is put to the traditional concept of a school as a consumer unit, an ivory tower [far removed] from

---

22. Lin Piao is reported to have advanced much the same argument in assessing losses and gains during the Cultural Revolution. See T'ung Hsin-kan, "United Action Committee Protects Privileged Class," *Ch'un-lei (Spring Thunder)*, Peking, published by the Revolutionary Rebel United General Headquarters of the Capital's 1 August School of Mao Tse-tung's Thought, July 1967.

social life. Our policy bridges the gap between educational and production units.[23]

University admissions policies were quickly changed to provide greater representation of secondary-level students from the countryside and from working-class families. Politics were stressed over academic work. Furthermore, in order to break down the traditional disdain of Chinese intellectuals for manual labor and manual laborers, students were "sent down" to work in the countryside (*hsiafang*).[24] Small factories and backyard iron smelters were allocated to schools to be manned by the students and faculty. Results of the Educational Revolution at Tsinghua University were described as follows:

Students spend one-third of a term in productive labor without affecting the fundamental courses. Each department will divide the time between theoretical teaching and productive labor in accordance with the characteristics of its specialization. Students in the departments of water conservation, engineering, and civil engineering generally spend one term in concentrated productive labor and two semesters in theoretical study. Other departments spend alternate days in work and in study, or work two days and study four days a week, or work half a day and study half a day. There is no standard method or sharp division. Some theoretical teaching is also carried out during the period of concentrated productive labor and some work is done during the period of concentrated theoretical teaching.

Since the half-work, half-study system has been in effect, politics remains a required course for all students. Every department will use two weeks of every school year for rectification of thinking and style of work.[25]

In Peking, the students' first big project was to help construct the Ming Tomb Reservoir. According to Morris Wills, an American student at Peita during this period, the students

---

23. *China Reconstructs,* VIII, No. 2, February 1959.
24. One student, a doctor's daughter educated by Canadian nuns, tells at length of her enthusiasm for *lao-tung* (physical labor of this kind) in Jan Myrdal's *Report from a Chinese Village* (New York: New American Library, 1966), pp. 344-351.
25. NCNA, November 1, 1958.

derived a "real sense of accomplishment" from their work. In July 1958, students were asked to set up small workshops, blast furnaces, and repair shops. In the fall, Peita students called off classes for a month to build a swimming pool. In September, with the start of the Steel Campaign, student volunteers left the university for the communes near Peking to help set up blast furnaces.

The Great Leap was characterized by enthusiasm and optimism and was a period when "most of the students believed in the campaign launched by the Party. They felt that the cause of communism was good and they considered themselves a part of it."[26] The students' support for the Great Leap and the Educational Revolution stands in sharp contrast to their bitter criticism of the Party during the Hundred Flowers campaign. (A group of these young students would later form the core of the leftist opposition that was to launch the Cultural Revolution at Peking University in 1966, by which time they were instructors and research assistants.) But at the highest level of the Party these vigorous revolutionary policies did not go unopposed.

---

26. Morris Wills (unpublished manuscript, Harvard University, 1965), pp. 83-88.

2

Elitism and the Growth of Left-Wing Opposition

To our knowledge, a balanced overall account of the Great Leap Forward, drawing on the important information made public during the Cultural Revolution, has not yet been published. In any case, it is important to bear in mind that China's Left, led by Mao, has rested an important part of its political case on the achievements of the Great Leap.[1] Opposition to the radical policies of the Great Leap soon developed, however. Right-wing attacks were typified by Defense Minister P'eng Teh-huai's "Letter of Opinion" of July 14, 1959. Four days after this letter was sent to Mao, Khrushchev attacked China's communes in a speech in Poland, but the plenary session of the Chinese Communist Party's Central Committee meeting in August 1959 proceeded to condemn the Defense Minister's views. In voting to dismiss him from this and other posts (although allowing him to remain a member of the Central Committee), it adopted, as was to be revealed later, a resolution setting forth these views on P'eng's position:

---

1. Anna Louise Strong's articles, collected in *The Rise of the Chinese People's Communes—and Six Years After* (Peking: New World Press, 1964), provide a vivid grass-roots account of the commune movement. She argues that the communes were essential for the prevention of mass starvation during the Three Hard Years (1960–1962), when the effects of large-scale natural calamities were exacerbated by the sudden withdrawal of Soviet aid.

P'eng Teh-huai has collected those transient and partial short-comings which have either long since been or are rapidly being overcome, exaggerated them out of all proportion and painted a pitch-black picture of the present situation in the country. In essence he negates the victory of the general line and the achievements of the Great Leap Forward, and is opposed to the high-speed development of the national economy, to the movement for high yields on the agricultural front, to the mass movement to make iron and steel, to the people's commune movement, to the mass movements in economic construction, and to Party leadership in socialist construction, that is, to "putting politics in command." In his letter he brazenly slandered as "petty-bourgeois fanaticism" the revolutionary zeal of the Party and of hundreds of millions of people. Time and again in his remarks he went so far as to assert that "if the Chinese workers and peasants were not as good as they are, a Hungarian incident would have occurred in China and it would have been necessary to invite Soviet troops in."[2]

Although in 1966 pessimistic assessments of the Great Leap were to be emphatically rejected by the rebel students, many of whom had themselves participated in construction projects or lived with peasant families proud of their achievements during this period, at this time a small group of academic figures and Party administrators in the cultural sphere publicly supported P'eng's attack, although in veiled terms. In 1965 Wu Han, an historian and vice-mayor of Peking, was to be accused of belonging to this rightist group. In June 1959 he had published an essay on Hai Jui, an "honest official" under the Ming Dynasty who was dismissed for criticizing the emperor. In what was taken, at least later, to be a direct attack on Mao, Wu Han quoted Hai Jui as telling the emperor that "present taxes and labor levies are abnormally high . . . these ten years or more have been chaotic. . . . You think you alone are right, you refuse to accept criticism and your mistakes are many. . . . This is the most serious problem in the country."[3] Two years

2. NCNA, August 15, 1967. See also K. H. Fan, *The Chinese Cultural Revolution: Selected Documents* (New York: Monthly Review Press, 1968).

3. *Jen-min Jih-pao* (*People's Daily*), June 16, 1959. Wu Han later argued that he was really attacking the rightists in his Hai Jui essays. The final paragraph of his essay in the *People's Daily* of September

later, Wu Han wrote a play called "Hai Jui Dismissed from Office," in which he is generally held to have been attacking the dismissal of P'eng Teh-huai. He also appears to advocate returning the land to private farming.

Although opinions like these were probably not widespread, they clearly had an influence on Peking intellectual circles, and they do not seem to have been repudiated by Peking's mayor, P'eng Chen. Such attitudes made it easier for various rightist officials to entrench themselves in the educational and cultural administrations.

In this new climate, much of China's Educational Revolution began to be slowly undermined. Reforms were criticized, particularly by professors and university presidents, for "lowering the quality of academic life"; many demanded a concerted effort to raise academic and professional standards. On the whole, this effort was supported by most high Party officials, and the Party adopted the slogan "advancing science" in the higher education system.

In 1959, Lu P'ing, the newly appointed Peking University president and secretary of the University's Party Committee, criticized the effects of the Educational Revolution:

The university must avoid and overcome the impetuous greediness for quantity and size and impatience for success, as well as the tendency toward unwillingness to bear hardships, to act realistically, and to do concrete work. Lofty revolutionary ambitions and big long-term targets of struggle must rest on a prac-

---

19, 1959, does indeed appear to attack "those who call themselves Hai Juis...but...devote themselves to opposing good men and good deeds saying, 'this is premature, it's too fast. ...'" But it must be noted that this was written after P'eng had clearly lost the argument for the time being. In addition, an examination of Wu Han's writings and deeds in the 1940's shows that he had a lengthy history of supporting the Kuomintang, although from a liberal standpoint, in its campaigns against the "Red bandits." He was still advocating liberal parliamentarianism in 1948, and said that the future of China rested with the enlightened intelligentsia.

See "Chronology of Wu Han's Anti-Communist, Anti-People, Counter-Revolutionary Activities in the Forties," *Kuang-ming Jih-pao* (Peking), May 6, 1966; *Survey of China Mainland Press*, No. 3709, pp. 10-25 (hereinafter cited as SCMP).

tical base of current concrete work. Otherwise they would simply be illusions. We must combine these ambitions with the good academic tradition of learning with realism and perseverance.[4]

Lu's plea for "realism" sounded sensible, and at that time such a corrective was probably needed. Lu seemed to be affirming the "red and expert" principle—i.e., that one should be both a good revolutionary and well trained in one's field—when he called for the integration of "lofty revolutionary ambitions" with "the good academic tradition of learning": "one must not stand the two in opposition to each other."[5]

But in the years immediately preceding the Cultural Revolution, Lu's work as an efficient and competent administrator of the prevailing educational policies gradually undercut whatever revolutionary zeal he may have had. As University president, he began more and more to take as his own the values cherished by university administrators in the Soviet Union and the West. As he became increasingly involved in strictly administrative affairs, his institutional role began to mold his political views and actions. As a proud alumnus of Peita, Lu P'ing's ambition was to establish it as a first-rate institution according to Soviet and Western standards.

Lu admired the success of Soviet industrialization, and for this reason he supported the application of the Soviet industrial experience to the task of modernizing China. He was quick to perceive the central role of the managerial and technical intelligentsia in the industrialization of the Soviet Union. In February 1962, at a meeting of University Party cadres, Lu is said to have declared:

The Soviet education system is a success. . . . Its space ships flew to the sky. We mustn't [let anything] shake our determination to learn well from the Soviet Union. . . . In operating schools we first have to turn to the Soviet Union for experience. We should learn from the Soviet system of education, and study education in Britain and the United States for reference.[6]

---

4. Wills, *op. cit.*, p. 94.
5. *Ibid.*
6. Chang En-ts'u, *Chung-kuo Ch'ing-nien Pao* (Peking), June 23, 1966; *SCMP* No. 3733.

In order to "produce useful people," Lu came to see
the purpose of Chinese higher education as training highly
skilled technocrats, and to this end he sought to model Peita
on Moscow University:[7] Peita, because of its "history and
status, . . . must always take a step ahead of others. This is
a heavy responsibility we must shoulder. We must catch up
with and surpass Moscow University. We must take Moscow
University as the target."[8]

In order to reach the high standards set at Moscow University, Lu stressed the development of "professionalism" among
the Party cadres assigned to Peita. According to Morris Wills,
the pressure to achieve professionalism led to a decline in Party
morale. Less educated cadres, many of whom were peasant
revolutionaries who had joined the Party during the Yenan
period, became intimidated. They felt that they lacked adequate
academic training to offer leadership. Party intellectuals in turn
tended to neglect Party work in order to concentrate on their
careers and professional advancement.[9] The professional ability
of applicants for Party membership became increasingly important, and political qualifications were correspondingly considered less necessary. As a result, Party recruitment campaigns
in the University led to admitting many new members who
excelled in academic work but lacked real political experience
and commitment. According to Wills, these new members "pre-
tended sincerity" but actually "joined the Party for personal
gain." The majority of them came from bourgeois backgrounds
and many were the sons and daughters of high officials and
military officers.[10]

Because they were more proficient administratively and
academically, these new members drew political responsibility
and power away from the older revolutionary cadres. In short,
the Party recruitment campaign at Peita resulted in the merging

7. K'ung Fan, "Lu P'ing's Revisionist Educational Line and Its Evil
   Consequences," *Jen-min Jih-pao* (Peking), July 19, 1966; *SCMP*
   No. 3751.
8. Chang En-ts'u, *loc. cit.*
9. Wills, *op. cit.*, p. 42.
10. *Ibid.*, pp. 47-48.

of political and intellectual elites. The new Party members had not been through the long revolutionary struggle which had forged the political identity of the older Party cadres. They had not experienced the solidarity, the egalitarian spirit, the commitment to political work, and the readiness for self-sacrifice—in short, the revolutionary élan—which characterized the years of hardship before 1949. These new men were committed to economic and social progress as they envisaged it, but tended to ignore political class struggle in favor of a vague rationalist humanism.

Prior to the Great Leap, Party members had primarily concentrated on overall decision-making, on mobilizing popular effort, and on the critical supervision of administration. Administration itself was left to administrators, who were often not Party members. The Great Leap, however, emptied many administrative offices, sending workers to the countryside to remold their world-outlook through physical labor. Party members were assigned to many of these administrative posts.

The pressures of professionalism, the influx of the new Party members, and the involvement of Party workers in routine administration combined to increase greatly the trend toward bureaucratization which had already set in. Administrative responsibility at Peita was transferred to the University Party Committee, headed by Lu P'ing. And the Party Committee, devoting its attention to administrative duties, grew increasingly isolated from the lower echelons of the Party organization, from the faculty, and particularly from the student body.

The University Party Committee was reluctant, or it was indifferent, to working closely with the student branches. It considered itself a higher organ of the Party and so preferred to work through the general branch. Also, the teachers' branches were obviously more important administratively. Many of the members of the Party general branch committees were teachers of the department, and they were the people who effectively controlled and ran the department. Anything the school Party Committee wanted accomplished among the students they could achieve through the teachers' branches and the general branch. There existed a hierarchy, with the school Party Committee at the top, then the Party branches, then the teachers, and last the student branches.[11]

As for the professors, Lu P'ing instructed them to devote themselves to raising their professional standards. He is said to have introduced in 1962 a plan which defined a strict status hierarchy and a system for the promotion of assistant lecturers, lecturers, associate professors, and professors based primarily on academic standards; political requirements were minimized. "Anyone may have his academic rank elevated if he is not politically against the Party and socialism."[12] Lu P'ing's encouragement of purely academic virtues and the system of ranks and promotion led to a growing tendency among Peita professors to "stress professionalism and treat politics lightly, to stress improving one's professional level and treat teaching lightly," and because the system favored competitive, research-oriented intellectuals, the great majority of new faculty members came from bourgeois backgrounds.[13] Lu also prodded his students to excel academically, insisting that students make up classes missed because of political activity. Students were instructed that their first duty was to study and to acquire professional ability.

Whether or not more expertise was in fact acquired, the consequences of the campaign to raise academic standards were immediately apparent in the political realm. Political activity declined sharply, both because it was discouraged by the university administration and because the heavy academic burden simply did not allow time for students to become involved in politics. Lu P'ing disbanded groups of students who formed seminars to study the political works of Mao, arguing that this "interfered with serious study."[14] One "political activist" from another school announced: "You can hardly make a living by counting on politics alone. Don't move about here and there. If you are not professionally sound, even the general Party

---

11. *Ibid.*, p. 30.
12. *Jen-min Jih-Pao* (Peking), July 19, 1966.
13. Wills, *op. cit.*, p. 42.
14. *Ibid.*, p. 53.

branch cannot do much in keeping you."[15]

At Peita the result was that "a lot of the comrades buried themselves in their books and grew indifferent to political activities," particularly the more ambitious students who wanted to make the most of their academic training. The popular phrase among these students was: "Become Einstein the Second." They felt that they had to "establish a name for themselves before the age of thirty."[16]

The educational system tended to make students compete among themselves for elite positions. Values and ways of thinking were bound to begin changing: a student would think less about the revolution and more about his career; less along egalitarian lines and more in elitist categories. Earlier commitments to go where the work was hardest and build a modern society in China's vast hinterland began to be superseded by thoughts of individual security and prestige as a future notable.

In this highly academic setting, the students who had been recruited from the countryside were left in much the same position as some of the first black students from the southern United States recruited into the Eastern Ivy League universities—they felt intimidated, "intellectually inferior," and culturally backward. Their classroom experiences must have been humiliating since they simply could not compete on the same

15. "The Black Program for Fostering Intellectual Aristocrats," *Hsin-hua Kung-pao* (Canton), SCMP No. 4128.

16. Wills, *op. cit.*, pp. 23, 41, 99. It seems that parents often exerted pressure on their children to propel them toward "great achievements," as defined by traditional values. One story tells of a landlord's daughter who confessed: "I passed the entrance examination for the T'ai-lai Middle School No. 1 after I was graduated from a higher primary school in the autumn of 1959. . . . My mother said to me more than once: 'You must study hard. You'll enter a senior middle school and then a university. After graduation from the university you will leave the countryside to become a doctor and a cadre. What a comfortable life it will be.' My mother's words struck root in my innermost soul. I spent the next three years studying with her words in mind. After my graduation from the junior middle school, however, I failed to gain admission to a senior middle school. When I returned home, my mother said to me: 'Alas, you, the daughter of a landlord, have returned to suffer at the hands of the dictatorship!' I also thought, 'farm work is dirty and tiresome. Can I stand it?' "

terms as the bourgeois students whose class position had provided obvious cultural and intellectual advantages. Professors nevertheless grew "impatient, and attacked slow students for their stupidity," looking on them as an "obstacle to academic quality."[17] A great number of these students were soon expelled or strongly urged to leave.

One of these students, Juang Chi-kuang, later wrote about his experience at Wuhan University.[18] His story reveals something of the complexity of the situation and provides an insight into the problems inherent in China's educational revolution.

Juang joined the 8th Route Army in 1948. In 1951 he went to Korea to fight with the People's Volunteer Army, and in 1955 he was assigned to a small government post in the countryside. He said that at that time "my cultural level was very low, so the Party sent me to the school for cultural cadres."[19] In 1959 Juang was assigned to the philosophy department at Wuhan University, where he became the secretary of his class's branch committee. During the Great Leap Forward he helped to write textbooks on philosophy "which

17. Wills, *op. cit.,* p. 41.
18. Chu Shao-t'ien, president of Wuhan University, was later to be accused by the Red Guards of: (1) Sabotaging the 1958 Education Revolution. He closed down the factories built in 1958 by faculty and students. He directed students to spend less time in productive labor and more in academic pursuits. (2) Firing and expelling "some of the most revolutionary people who had entered the university during the Great Leap who were backward and not interested in academic work." (3) Reorganizing the Party apparatus at the school to eliminate the cadres who had come to power during the Great Leap and who refused to cooperate with his program which stressed academic work. "He readjusted, transferred out, and changed on a large scale, the backbone elements of the 1958 Educational Revolution, and planted his own intimates on the Party Committee and in key positions in the departments." (4) Dissolving the school affairs committee and the department affairs committees organized by "the revolutionary faculty and students in 1958" and "setting up new committees drawing from professors and conservative elements." Thus he resembled Lu P'ing in his conception of what a university should be like. *Ch'ing-kang Hsueh-pao* (Wuhan), June 25, 1966. See also Wills, *op. cit.,* pp. 96-98.
19. Most of the following is taken from *Hung-wei Pao* (Canton), September 8, 1966.

applied the mass line approach to education." But in 1961

Li Ta, Chu Shao-t'ien and Ho Ting-hua [embers of the administration] sneaked into the Party to take advantage of the situation and to seize the leadership of Wuhan University. They beat down the revolutionary Left, carried to the platform bourgeois specialists and "professors." They openly yelled that in the past "there was too much revolution and teaching was placed in a passive position," with the result that the university does not look like a university at all. . . . Being a revolutionary cadre, I could not waver in face of the attack by the bourgeoisie. . . . So I led my fellow students of the whole class to participate conscientiously in various kinds of labor inside the university compound, such as collecting manure and growing vegetables. This was aimed at cultivating habits of doing labor enthusiastically and a style of simple living and hard work.

But with the "trimming" of the programs of the Great Leap Forward, Juang was instructed by the school administration to stop leading his students out into the fields. Juang reluctantly consented to this, but responded: "As far as I myself was concerned, I would forget my origin and degenerate if I did not labor. In the early morning and after supper I would go out to labor and other students would follow me." When he persisted in this course, Ho Ting-hua, a school administrator, called a general meeting of the University and publicly criticized Juang for being "a bad student who did nothing but labor, did not study seriously, and exerted an extremely bad influence." Despite this criticism, Juang remained convinced that what he had done conformed to Chairman Mao's ideas on education and to the Party's educational policy. "Gradually," he wrote, "I felt that Li Ta and company did not want us to study and apply Chairman Mao's works creatively in the course of struggle and labor and to become staunch revolutionary fighters. They wanted to train us into a special stratum divorced from labor and riding on the backs of the people." Juang continued his demand that "education be integrated with productive labor," but he was repeatedly turned down. He continues:

It was only after repeated prompting from us students that in 1961 the Li Ta black gang felt compelled to agree to our going to the countryside to make social surveys. Before our departure, in a "directive" to the Party branch of our class, they said: "The purpose of the present trip is mainly to collect data for future scientific research." This was an attempt to prevent us from engaging in productive labor. With resolution we went to the countryside to participate in labor, practiced the Three Togethernesses [living, eating, and talking with the peasants], cultivated class feelings in ourselves, transformed our world outlook, and achieved the revolutionization of our thinking.

In response to the renewed emphasis on raising academic standards at Wuhan University, Juang wrote:

Li Ta and company—bourgeois lords who entrenched themselves in Wuhan University—regarded the worker and peasant cadres and students who persevered in the revolutionary direction as the greatest obstacle to their executing the bourgeois and revisionist line on education. They looked upon me as a difficult to handle, "bad" student. In all sorts of ways they used the old teaching system—a most sinister tactic—to persecute me. When the implementation of the "less but finer" principle was called for, the Department of Philosophy nevertheless carried out the "extensive and broad knowledge" policy; with the Li Ta black gang boasting that philosophy was a comprehensive science, they set up in the Department of Philosophy courses on mathematics, chemistry, biology, aesthetics, foreign languages, as well as the history of Chinese philosophy, the history of foreign philosophies, the history of modern China, modern world history, psychology, and logic, exceeding twenty in number. . . .

These courses contained ancient and foreign things, things feudal, capitalistic, and revisionist. They sought everywhere a number of "bourgeois specialists" and invited them to the university to "lecture" in order to spread poison. Works by Chairman Mao were regarded as "reference" books.

Juang found this development to be "intolerable":

At first I demanded that these courses which led one to separate oneself from the class struggle be suspended, but they refused to do so. . . . I felt strongly that if things went on like this, not only could I not master the thought of Mao Tse-tung, but my own revolutionary will would be sapped and my revolutionary soul would be corrupted. I felt that such a university was not a crucible for revolutionization. . . . I felt that I could not remain here any longer.

In 1964 Juang decided to ask that he be allowed to withdraw from the university. He went to Ho Ting-hua's house to tell him of his decision. "He of course welcomed the idea of such a stupid student like me leaving the university."

One of the major accomplishments of the Great Leap Forward had been the massive school construction program launched throughout the country to provide the infrastructure for eventual universal education. The greatest emphasis was placed on establishing new schools in the countryside, particularly at the primary and junior middle school level, though many senior middle schools were also constructed.

Because of China's severely limited capital and an equally severe shortage of teachers, the quality of these new schools was generally low. Most of them operated on a part-time basis as half-work, half-study schools where students studied in the morning and worked in the afternoons. The self-sufficient agricultural middle schools constructed by local villagers for peasant children at the junior middle school level were schools of this kind. The students helped pay operating costs by contributing their labor.[20]

In contrast to the half-work, half-study schools were the full-time schools, located mainly in the cities. Their students not only could study on a full-time basis, but also had access to better physical facilities, libraries, and teachers. It was natural that students attending these schools had a marked advantage over half-work, half-study students in the quality of their primary and secondary education; and, partly in consequence, they had a greater opportunity to go on to the university.

20. See Robert D. Barendsen, "Agricultural Middle School in Communist China," in Roderick MacFarquhar's *China Under Mao, op cit.,* pp. 304-322.

Admission into secondary and higher education before the Cultural Revolution was based on three criteria—the applicant's class background, political record, and performance on entrance examinations. Although the applicant's class background and political record were important factors, the emphasis from 1959 on was increasingly shifted to a competitive system based on the applicant's performance on the entrance examination. These examinations were administered once a year in June to students applying for admission to junior middle schools, senior middle schools, and the universities. Competition grew as the student climbed the ladder; only one out of ten applicants was accepted into senior middle school, and at the university level the odds against admission were reported to be thirty to one.[21]

Those defending the examinations claimed that they provided a fair and uniform admissions system which selected the most capable students for further training. But inherent in the system were considerable inequities: rural applicants and those who had attended half-work, half-study schools were immediately at a disadvantage; the system favored students who had attended full-time schools in the cities, or children of cadres who had studied at special boarding schools. Students from privileged positions in society—children of high Party officials, and of the old bourgeois and landlord classes—were therefore favored. But some officials still were not satisfied with this degree of selectivity. Lu Ting-yi is reported to have attacked the Educational Revolution as early as 1959, saying it had generally lowered the quality of education.[22]

An important question which arises is whether standards in specialized instruction at the top of the educational pyramid really declined in absolute terms, or whether there was merely a "deterioration" in the averages on paper owing to the rapid increase in the number of hitherto neglected students. In any case, in 1962 Lu is reported to have issued a directive to all

21. *Yomiuri,* June 25, 1966, in *Daily Survey of the Japanese Press,* June 20-29, 1966.
22. *Jen-min Jih-pao,* December 17, 1967, *SCMP* No. 4100.

provinces and municipalities outlining a program to "elevate" the quality of education. Directors of education at the provincial and municipal levels were called on to select a number of "key schools" from among the universities, secondary schools, and primary schools. In May 1963 directors of educational bureaus at the provincial level met at a special conference in which plans were drawn up to establish a system of elite schools: 235 secondary schools (25 percent of all the full-time secondary schools) and 1,472 primary schools (31 percent of all the full-time primary schools) were selected. "From these schools they again carefully picked 36 secondary schools and 162 primary schools" as the best of the elite schools, and decided to concentrate manpower and material resources on these.[23]

By 1965 China's educational system looked something like this: At the top were all of the elite schools, which were to train students for the universities. Their students were to become China's future leaders, scientists, and professional men. Below the elite schools were the general full-time schools, which were to train middle-level technicians, engineers, and teachers, most of whom were destined for positions in the countryside. At the bottom were the part-time schools—the half-work, half-study schools—which were there to provide a minimal education for China's future peasant and working classes; they were also to train lower-level technicians and engineers to staff the modernization projects in the countryside.

It was this hierarchy, and particularly its elite component, which was to be attacked by the Red Guards during the Cultural Revolution. Seeking to eliminate institutional sources of privilege, students of the Red Guard Corps of the 4th Middle School in Peking, one of the city's ten "key-point" schools, criticized their school because of its "superior material conditions," and the "spiritual aristocratic" attitude many students developed while studying there. They argued that "China's Khrushchev [Liu Shao-ch'i] divided our schools into two categories. One category was to train mental workers. Students from this category would be cadres, engineers, writers, artists,

---

23. *Ibid.*

theoreticians, educators, etc. The other category was to train
physical laborers. Students from this category would be workers, peasants, service personnel, etc." Students admitted into the
4th Middle School "would not go to rural areas and be peasants after they left school." In this sense, "the old educational
system produced on the one hand mental laborers who 'ruled
people' and on the other hand physical laborers who were
'ruled.' "[24] One is reminded here of a well-known passage from
Mencius on the difference between those who think and those
who toil:

Great men have their proper business, and little men have
their proper business. . . . Some labor with their minds, and some
labor with their strength. Those who labor with their minds govern others; those who labor with their strength are governed by
others. Those who are governed by others support them, those
who govern others are supported by them.[25]

The hierarchical system threatened to perpetuate structures
which could only reinforce the social values of traditional China,
where a good education provided the basis of power and
prestige. At the same time, the system incalculated the values of
a new technocratic ethos similar to that of the Soviet Union:

Why were there always people who would try to get their
children into the 4th Middle School or some other "key" middle
school by all available means? Simply because they wanted their
children to enter a university. In their eyes that particular university was a cradle of engineers, while the 4th Middle School
was an "affiliated school" of the university. It was a "short cut"
to a high position.[26]

The best of the elite schools were the boarding schools for
children of Party officials. These were originally intended to
care for and educate the children of cadres during the Civil

---

24. Red Guard Corps of the 4th Middle School of Peking, "Five Major
    Charges Against the Old Education System," *Jen-min Jih-pao*, Decem-
    ber 17, 1967.
25. Cited in Etienne Belaz, *Chinese Civilization and Bureaucracy* (New
    Haven: Yale University Press, 1964), p. 17.
26. "Five Major Charges . . .", *op. cit.*

War, when cadres were engaged in revolutionary activity which separated them from their children.[27] But after the defeat of the Kuomintang, these schools increasingly came to be exclusive schools for the children of a new ruling elite, the higher cadres of the Chinese Communist Party. This became particularly apparent after 1962 when, as a part of the elite school program, the "collective boarding schools" were selected to be developed into China's finest primary and secondary schools.

During the Cultural Revolution these collective boarding schools were to be attacked by Red Guards for being similar to the British and Soviet "schools for aristocratic children." Though rhetorically exaggerated, this criticism was firmly grounded in reality. As institutions, these schools differed but little from the preparatory schools for the children of the ruling classes in the West. Students attending these schools appear to have felt that because their parents had been revolutionary leaders (at least at one time), they were bound to follow in their footsteps, even if they were rarely to leave a comfortable office in Peking. Given the orientation of their education, their privileged position, and their family background, it is easy to imagine that many children of high officials might, especially in a third generation, develop the arrogance and self-assertiveness which characterize the offspring of ruling classes elsewhere.[28] The students had been told in essence that "in the future you should become generals, ministers, and prime ministers. You are the hard core of the successors [to revolutionary leadership] and should not go around selling soy and vinegar." And, in fact, during the 1950's and early 1960's only a very few graduates of the quality schools were assigned to work in the countryside.[29]

---

27. "Oppose Collective Boarding Schools for Children of Cadres," *Ch'un-lei (Spring Thunder)*, No. 4, April 13, 1967. This article is reproduced below in the Appendix.
28. *Ibid.*
29. *Ibid.*

Although the leftists were generally beaten down after the cutback in the Great Leap program, those who remained in the universities continued to agitate in whatever way they could. At Peita they continued to press for the enrollment of more students from worker-peasant backgrounds, for more time for political study, and for the continuation of the work projects begun during the Great Leap, if only in limited form.[30] Tense relations between the University's bureaucrats and the leftist students and young instructors persisted throughout the period between the Great Leap and the Cultural Revolution.

But it was the bureaucrats who had the upper hand, and they fulfilled "Maoist" demands only at a token level. Lu P'ing's response to the proliferation of school workshops during the Great Leap was to complain: "So many factories have been established in the school! Shall I be director of a school or of a factory?" He then proceeded to have them closed down, one after another, although he did keep a few open as "model workshops."[31] He felt that the work-study program interfered with academic pursuits, and therefore reduced the time students spent on productive labor to one month per year. Moreover, students were given trivial job assignments within the University compound, so that "during the time of labor there was no emphasis on going to the factories and the countryside, no emphasis on integration of the students with the workers and peasants, and no emphasis on ideological remolding."[32] Above all, the enrollment of students from worker or peasant families at Peita was sharply reduced, from 66.8 percent in 1960 to 37.7 percent in 1962.[33]

After a Central Committee plenum in 1962, however, when Mao gained rather grudging support for a movement

30. Wills, *op. cit.*, pp. 86-102.
31. *Ibid.*, p. 91.
32. K'ung Fan, *Jen-min Jih-pao* (Peking), July 19, 1966; *SCMP* No. 3751.
33. Ione Kramer in *Progressive Labor*, Vol. 6, No. 2 (November-December 1967). Kramer is an American writer living in China. According to A. Jackson-Thomas and his co-authors, at one point only 20 percent of the students admitted were from such backgrounds. (See "How It All Started.")

known as the Socialist Education Campaign, aimed primarily at re-consolidating the collective economy in the countryside, students went to the countryside as members of "work teams," and assisted in the campaign to check the spontaneous tendencies toward capitalism in the villages—the increase in private plots, excessive sideline occupations, rural free markets, the tendency among better-off peasants to "go it alone," and the re-emergence of rich peasants. They were instructed to assist poorer families in class struggle by helping to organize poor and lower-middle peasant associations (representing about 60 to 70 percent of the rural population), which then held meetings to criticize the growth of corruption among cadres.

At the same time, demands for more radical policies within and outside the universities became more insistent and frequent. The Socialist Education Campaign was brought to the cities on a limited scale, and in October 1964 it came to Peita. A work team arrived to carry out a rectification of the school's Party apparatus. "The work team led meetings [which appear to have been limited to Party members] in every Faculty where those Party members in authority who were taking the capitalist road were exposed." Lu P'ing apparently feared that his position and that of his associates was being undermined for the Peking Municipal Committee under P'eng Chen, with which Lu had close ties, immediately summoned the work team and criticized it for not following its own directives. Work team members were accused of making "reckless" attacks, and in March and April 1965 the Municipal Committee organized "struggle" meetings to force the work team members to admit mistakes. When they refused to accept criticism, the Municipal Committee then instructed the work team to leave the campus "on the pretext that the summer holidays were approaching." The Municipal Committee apparently felt their own position would be endangered if Lu P'ing were compromised.

Shortly after the recall of the work team, Lu P'ing ferreted out the Party members who had criticized his administration and sent about eighty of them off to the International Hotel in downtown Peking. There, for seven months (from July

1965 to January 1966), Lu P'ing's group tried to discredit the dissident Party members by getting them to admit that they were "careerists" and members of an "anti-Party clique."

The "rectification" session at the International Hotel "was organized in conjunction with the Municipal Committee," which assisted Lu P'ing in organizing two hundred University Party members to "struggle with the eighty." It was expected that these Party members would support Lu P'ing, "since the charges were that the victims were anti-Party"; but in fact "a number went over to the side of the eighty." Furthermore, "in reporting events to the Central Committee, the Peking Municipal Committee sorted and rearranged the facts to their own advantage. During these months a small number of those under fire submitted, but most stood firm."[34]

One member of this International Hotel group was Nieh Yuan-tzu, an instructor in the department of philosophy. During 1961–1962, she had been chosen Party secretary of the department's branch committee over the incumbent backed by Lu P'ing. This followed a sharp dispute in 1958 in the department over the Three Red Banners (the general line, the Great Leap, and the communes). Nieh reports that Lu P'ing, despite his normal aversion to physical labor for university members, retaliated by "sending many people to the country for 'labor duty' and 'keeping them there a long time.' "[35]

---

34. Most of the material for the preceding account comes from "How It All Started."

35. Interview with Nieh by Anna Louise Strong, reprinted in *Progressive Labor*, Vol. 6, No. 2 (November-December 1967), p. 75. Nieh also said that when members of the International Hotel group wrote a letter of protest to Mao, it was diverted "into the hands of their tormentors," and they thus came to recognize that P'eng Chen had the protection of even higher Party officials. On this point, an article in an unofficial Canton rebel newspaper, *Pa-erh-wu Chan-pao* (*August 25 Battle News*), February 14, 1967 (SCMP No. 574), says the following:

"In 1964, the Socialist Education Movement was launched in institutions of higher learning with Peking University as the experimental center. The teachers and students of Peking University exposed the counter-revolutionary clique headed by Lu P'ing, and began to make an investigation of the Peking Municipal Committee.

During this period from 1962 to 1965, the question of successors to the first generation of socialist revolutionaries became acute throughout China. In 1964, Mao Tse-tung offered these thoughts on this question; they were to be in the pockets of almost everyone in China two and a half years later:

Basing themselves on the changes in the Soviet Union, the imperialist prophets are pinning their hopes of "peaceful evolution" on the third or fourth generation of the Chinese Party. We must shatter these imperialist prophecies. From our highest organizations down to the grass-roots, we must everywhere give constant attention to the training and upbringing of successors to the revolutionary cause. . . .

They must be revolutionaries who wholeheartedly serve the overwhelming majority of the people of China and the whole world, and must not be like Khrushchev, who serves both the interests of the handful of members of the privileged bourgeois stratum in his own country and those of foreign imperialism and reaction.

They must be proletarian statesmen capable of uniting and working together with the overwhelming majority. Not only must they unite with those who agree with them, they must also be good at uniting with those who disagree and even with those who formerly opposed them and have since been proven wrong in practice. But they must especially watch out for careerists and

---

Liu Shao-ch'i and Teng Hsiao-p'ing promptly directed P'eng Chen to organize oppression. Teng Hsiao-p'ing also energetically backed up Lu P'ing, saying: 'Lu P'ing's attitude is good and his view is correct.'

"At the meeting of the Secretariat of the Central Committee held on March 3 in the same year, Teng Hsiao-p'ing also leveled three fabricated charges against Socialist Education work in Peking University: First, it had a wrong idea of the character of the problem, regarded the university as a rotten unit, and carried out a struggle to seize power; second, it did not carry out the three-way alliance; third, it erred seriously in the method of struggle and carried the struggle to excess. He venomously attacked the revolutionaries as 'opportunists using the shoulders of others as rungs to climb up the ladder.' On April 3, Teng Hsiao-p'ing ordered the replacement of Chang P'an-shih with Hsü Li-ch'un, a member of the black gang, as the leader of the work team.

"Because of this, Teng Hsiao-p'ing was the commander-in-chief of the seven month long counter-revolutionary incident in Peking University."

conspirators like Khrushchev and prevent such bad elements from usurping the leadership of the Party and the state at any level....

Successors to the revolutionary cause of the proletariat come forward in mass struggles and are tempered in the great storms of revolution. It is essential to test and judge cadres and choose and train successors in the long course of mass struggle.[36]

Among the campaigns to engage young people in public affairs were the campaign to learn from the poor and lower-middle peasants, the campaign to learn from the People's Liberation Army (PLA), and the campaign to emulate Lei Feng, Wang Chieh, and other PLA heroes. As we have mentioned, the Socialist Education Campaign provided special opportunities for students to participate in rural politics. The reasons for learning from the army and emulating soldiers may seem more obscure.

When P'eng Teh-huai was dismissed from his post as Defense Minister (see p. 25) in 1959, leadership of China's armed forces passed to Lin Piao, who had joined the then newly formed Communist Party on graduation from the famous Whampoa Military Academy at eighteen and had become a colonel in the original Kuomintang army before he was twenty. The leader of the Long March, Lin organized the Northwest Anti-Japanese Red Army University in Yenan, which attracted many students from the coastal cities to the revolutionary cause. The *Washington Post* (June 12, 1966) reported that he "has invariably been described as an able, gentle, studious man of unusual courage." Under Lin's guidance, the PLA has abolished ranks and ordered officers to serve as ordinary soldiers. Army documents, apparently seized by Tibetan rightists in an attack on a PLA regimental post in mid-1961 and swiftly turned over to the U.S. government, show how the PLA boldly used Mao's "mass line" to encourage "big contention, big blooming, big debate, and big-character posters" in the ranks and among the people as a means of helping to overcome the grave diffi-

36. Quoted in "On Khrushchev's Phoney Communism and Its Historical Lessons for the World" (July 14, 1964), reprinted in *Quotations from Chairman Mao Tse-tung* (Peking: Foreign Languages Press, 1966), pp. 277-279.

culties which the Chinese Revolution faced during the Three Hard Years.[37]

One of Lin Piao's major precepts in renovating the PLA was that men and their ideas were far more important than weapons. Wang Chieh, a twenty-three-year-old PLA squad leader who was killed when he threw his body over a defective mine to save the lives of the commune militia members he was teaching, is one of a number of ordinary soldiers, workers, and cadres who are cited as examples of a new socialist spirit of willing service and sacrifice for the common cause. Five months after Wang's death in July 1965, his diary was published and it was widely and enthusiastically read by students. Among the points Wang Chieh stresses are industry and frugality: "A drop of oil, a screw, a fuse, or an ounce of dynamite is the property of the nation and the people. . . . However little I can save, I will do my best to save for my country."[38] But Wang Chieh is no classical hero, with special natural endowments. On the contrary, he is perhaps of somewhat less than average physical strength and intelligence; what distinguishes him is his will to perfect himself in order to live up to his ideals, even at the expense of challenging established authority:

One winter night, [his] unit was sent out to build a bridge. There was a thin layer of ice on the river and chilling wind and rain struck down harder and harder. The company needed six strong men to work in the river. Wang Chieh wanted to, but the squad leader thought he was not strong enough, and therefore refused. He begged: "Squad leader, if you really want to make a good fighter of me, you must give me every opportunity to steel myself." Saying this, he took off his quilt tunic and jumped in the water before anyone else.[39]

---

37. These remarkable documents have now been published in translation in *The Politics of the Chinese Red Army: A Translation of the Bulletin of Activities of the People's Liberation Army*, ed. J. Chester Chen *et al.* (Stanford: Stanford University Press, 1966).

38. Wang Chieh's diary for March 5, 1964, cited in Mary Sheridan, "The Emulation of Heroes," *China Quarterly*, No. 33 (January-March 1968), p. 53.

39. *Chung-kuo Ch'ing-nien* (*Chinese Youth*), No. 22 (1965), cited in Mary Sheridan's article, p. 56.

Despite the appearance of figures like Wang Chieh, Mao Tse-tung was far from certain that the new generations were receiving sufficient education in revolutionary politics. In January 1965 he remarked to Edgar Snow that those under twenty had never fought a war, seen an imperialist, or known capitalism in power. Parents could tell them about such things, "but to hear about history and to read books was not the same thing as living it." Still, Mao seemed quite philosophically detached about this in light of the events to come. In his view,

future events would be decided by future generations, and in accordance with conditions we could not foresee. . . . The youth of today and those to come after them would assess the work of the Revolution in accordance with values of their own. Mao's voice dropped away, and he half closed his eyes. Man's condition on this earth was changing with ever increasing rapidity. A thousand years from now all of them, he said, even Marx, Engels, and Lenin, would possibly appear rather ridiculous.[40]

But 1965 was the year of massive American intervention in Vietnam.

---

40. Edgar Snow, "Interview with Mao," *New Republic*, January 20, 1965; reprinted in Franz Schurmann and Orville Schell, *The China Reader: Communist China* (New York: Vintage Books, 1967), pp. 359-375.

3

The Cultural Revolution
Comes to Peita

The possibility of war in mid-1965 seems to have led some high Chinese Party officials to rely more and more on broadened and tightened centralized controls to meet the new circumstances. In doing so, they probably hoped to strengthen "national unity," and the hasty admission of about eight million new members to the Communist Youth League, including many from bourgeois and landlord families, was apparently a reflection of this attitude. Class struggles and revolutionary politics were minimized, even though the influence of the national bourgeoisie was still quite strong in China's cities, and the livelihood of the poorer peasant households was jeopardized by threats to the collective rural economy.[1]

Mao, on the other hand, believed that in case of war and a deep enemy penetration into China, it would be essential to rely on the most revolutionary classes in society, those which had proven most energetic in resisting the Japanese invaders. If preparation against war was needed, it should not lead to neglecting the poorer classes in the name of "unity," or affording the bourgeoisie or former landlords special "bribes" for

---

1. A Japanese correspondent who visited the CYL Central Headquarters in October 1965 is said to have reported that the leaders there were very reluctant to discuss ideological questions. See *Tokyo Shimbun,* December 21, 1966, cited by John Israel in "The Red Guards in Historical Perspective: Continuity and Change in the Chinese Youth Movement," *China Quarterly,* No. 30 (April-June 1967), p. 4.

good behavior. It was therefore necessary to criticize and repudiate Wu Han, the author of "Hai Jui Dismissed from Office," and others who held positions of authority and most out-
spokenly opposed revolutionary policies: such men could not
be relied on if it should become necessary to fight a people's
war. The degree to which various leaders did in fact expect
war is of course a matter of speculation. Some foreign observers
have suggested that it is precisely because Mao did not expect
immediate full-scale war that he felt free to launch the criticism
of Wu Han. But it appears to us that as the problem became
acute Mao would in any case have opposed the trend toward
abandoning the reliance on the revolutionary classes and sub-
stituting organizational control from above for mass mobiliza-
tion at the grass roots. Mao raised the question of criticizing
Wu Han at a Central Committee working conference held in
September and October 1965.

At Peking University, meanwhile, the members of the
International Hotel group were still undergoing "criticism." It
is not clear how many other students were aware of what was
happening at the hotel. Marianne Bastid, a French student in
Chinese history at Peita from September 1964 to September
1966, appears to have known nothing of this incident.[2] But she
did become aware of a change in the political climate in September and October 1965. During September there were a
large number of political classes and meetings; in some courses,
no regular classes were held. Over the next month, two-thirds
of the University's members are said to have left for the countryside, some for communes near Peking, just beyond the Great
Wall, others for as far away as Szechwan. Bastid says the purpose of their mission was announced as being mainly to hold

---

2. Marianne Bastid's article, "Origines et développement de la révolution
culturelle," *Politique étrangère* (Paris), 32e année (1967), No. 1, pp.
68-86, is a particularly useful source for the period from September
1965 to August 1966. The article was completed on November 29,
1966. Our account of events at Peita follows her account fairly closely,
except where otherwise noted. We have also drawn on an interview
with Marianne Bastid by Victor Nee in the summer of 1968; information gleaned from this is noted separately.

political courses for the peasants and was different from the earlier "Four Clean-ups" phase of the Socialist Education movement. Although their stay was originally to last only two or three months, their return was postponed several times, and they did not in fact get back to the University until after the great events of late May 1966.

The decision for this massive departure was apparently quite sudden. Classes which had not been scheduled to leave received "marching orders" only forty-eight hours in advance. It seems possible, therefore, that the Peking Municipal Committee and Lu P'ing's administration already feared that their opponents within the University community—who had revealed themselves during the Socialist Education movement—might gain added strength during the campaign of criticism against Wu Han, deputy mayor under P'eng Chen. In any case, it is clear that the Peking Municipal Committee was alarmed by an article by Yao Wen-yuan criticizing "Hai Jui Dismissed from Office" which was published in Shanghai on November 10, even though this first article was mainly devoted to questioning the historical accuracy of Wu Han's portrayal of the Ming official Hai Jui and did not directly raise the question of whether it was P'eng Teh-huai's dismissal from office which was being described. P'eng Chen's associates are reported to have immediately phoned Shanghai complaining, "What right have you to publish Yao Wen-yuan's article? Why have you not notified us in advance? Where is your Party character?"[3]

A number of articles for and against Wu Han, including his own "self-criticism," were published during December and January, but by February 1966, according to Marianne Bastid, public attention was turning more and more to the danger of an expansion of the war in Vietnam. At Peita, the History Faculty and part of the Philosophy Faculty were moved to a state farm near the Ming Tombs in Peking's suburbs. There was much discussion of how education might be reformed along the lines of the wartime Anti-Japanese University in Yenan. In

---

3. Ch'i Pen-yu, "On the Bourgeois Stand of *Frontline* and the *Peking Daily*," *Hung-ch'i* (*Red Flag*), No. 7, May 11, 1966.

March, however, discussion of Wu Han again came to the fore, this time in a more distinctly political context, at least for readers of the national press outside Peking. Teng T'o, a secretary of the Peking Municipal Committee, had published a series of articles in 1961–1962 with Wu Han and Liao Mo-sha (director of the Committee's United Front Department) which were even more suspect than "Hai Jui." Now, apparently aware that he would come under fire for these articles, Teng T'o published his own "criticism" of the series on April 16 in an article in *Peking Daily,* which, however, attempted to avoid the real political issues.

That morning, at 6:00 A.M., the Peita Party Committee under Lu P'ing called a meeting of Party members and told them: "Today *Peking Daily* carries an important article and you are urged to study it seriously and pay attention to the reactions of the masses. When the paper is delivered, we will distribute it to you right away."[4] According to the same source, the Party Committee "had been silent for quite some time" before this early-morning meeting, and had not previously been actively engaged in distributing morning papers. In the afternoon, Lu P'ing called the first mass meeting to "criticize" Wu Han, and "personally guided a number of teachers and students of the Law Department in an examination of the data consisting of 14 million characters in 15 hundred volumes which dealt with the problem of how Hai Jui 'righted wrongs'. . . ."[5]

For the next month, Lu P'ing's administration attempted to confine discussion to an academic debate about Hai Jui's merits and Wu Han's portrayal of them. Even after a vigorous broadside against the publications controlled by the Peking Municipal Committee in the May 8 *Liberation Army Daily,* on May 14 Lu P'ing sent the Peita Party Committee a message from Sung Shuo, deputy director of the Universities Department of the Municipal Committee, which included the following instructions:

---

4. "How Lu P'ing Has Served 'Three-Family Village,'" an article whose authors seem to be Peita Party members, in *Jen-min Jih-pao (People's Daily),* June 5, 1966.

5. *Ibid.*

The anti-Party, anti-socialist remarks have to be completely repudiated theoretically. . . . This struggle must be conducted in a very careful manner. . . . The masses, when they arise, need to be led onto the correct path. . . . Only by energetically assuming the leadership can the movement be led to its normal development . . . big meetings can in no way serve to theoretically repudiate them.[6]

By this time, the members of the International Hotel group appear for the most part to have been allowed to return to the campus. The hotel bill, when the affair was wound up in January, amounted to some 200,000 yuan, and at that time only a few "tough nuts," mostly from the Philosophy Faculty, remained. Among the philosophy instructors left were Nieh Yuan-tzu, the department's Party Secretary, Sung I-hsiu, Hsia Chien-chia, Yang K'e-ming, Chao Cheng-yi, Kao Yun-p'eng, and Li Hsing-ch'en.[7]

On May 18, a confidential circular from the Central Committee arrived at the Peita campus and it became clear to Nieh Yuan-tzu, who was able to read it since she was a departmental secretary, that Lu P'ing's administration, in league with the Municipal Committee, had finally opened itself to attack for failing to permit full-scale criticism of Wu Han. Peking's Mayor P'eng Chen had clearly been allowed to dig his own political grave. The circular read:

The Central Committee has decided to revoke the "Outline Report on the Current Academic Discussion Made by the Group of Five in Charge of the Cultural Revolution" which was approved for distribution on February 12, 1966. . . .

The outline report by the so-called Group of Five is actually an outline report by P'eng Chen alone. . . . Employing the most improper methods, he acted arbitrarily, abused his powers and, usurping the name of the Central Committee, hurriedly issued the outline report to the whole Party. . . .

Instead of encouraging the entire Party boldly to arouse the broad masses of workers, peasants, and soldiers and the fighters for proletarian culture so that they can continue to charge ahead,

6. Cited in "How It All Started," p. 23.
7. *Ibid.*

the outline does its best to turn the movement to the Right. . . .
In particular, it obscures the aim of this great struggle, which is
to criticize and repudiate Wu Han and the considerable number
of other anti-Party and anti-socialist representatives of the bourgeoisie (there are a number of these in the Central Committee
and in the Party, government, and other departments at the central as well as at the provincial, municipal, and autonomous re-
gion levels).[8]

Nieh Yuan-tzu and the other six philosophy instructors
immediately began preparing a big-character poster criticizing
Lu P'ing, P'eng P'ei-yun (the Peita Party Committee's vice-
secretary), and Sung Shuo (from the Municipal Committee's
Universities Department). "We put up our poster on May 25
just after two o'clock on the outer wall of the University dining-
hall," Nieh later told Anna Louise Strong.[9] The poster was
entitled "What Have Sung Shuo, Lu P'ing, and P'eng P'ei-yun
Done in the Cultural Revolution?" It began by drawing attention to Sung Shuo's instructions delivered by Lu P'ing on May
14 and the manner in which Lu P'ing and P'eng P'ei-yun had
implemented them, and concluded:

Why are you so afraid of wall-posters in big characters?
Why are you afraid of holding condemnation meetings? To coun-
terattack the black gang which launched a frenzied attack against
the Party, socialism, and the thought of Mao Tse-tung is a life-
or-death class struggle. . . . To hold meetings and to post big-
character posters are mass militant styles of the best form. You
"lead" the masses not to hold meetings and not to put up big-
character posters. You have manufactured various taboos and
regulations. By so doing, have you not suppressed the mass revolution, forbidden it, and opposed it? We absolutely won't allow
you to do so![10]

---

8. Circular of May 16, 1966, published in *Peking Review*, May 19,
   1967. The Circular adds: "The outline violates the basic Marxist
   thesis that all class struggles are political struggles. When the press
   began to touch on the political issues involved in Wu Han's 'Hai Jui
   Dismissed from Office,' the authors of the outline went so far as to
   say: 'The discussion in the press should not be confined to political
   questions, but should go fully into the various academic and theoretical
   questions involved.' "
9. Interview with Nieh.
10. *Jen-min Jih-pao (People's Daily)*, June 2, 1966.

According to Jean-François Billeter, a Swiss student attending Peita at the time, the immediate reaction on the campus was stupefaction and total silence. Students then gathered in small groups, read the poster, whispered apprehensively to one another over its validity, and wondered what was to come next. Their conversation was marked above all by its cautious tone. But support soon began to materialize, and in a few hours the walls were covered with additional posters.[11] When Lu P'ing, who was attending a meeting of the old Municipal Party Committee, learned the news, he rushed back to the University to organize a last-ditch resistance.[12] According to Billeter, he did so by mobilizing members of the Communist Youth League, whose leadership was conservative since it was tied organizationally to Lu P'ing's administration. CYL members in turn put up posters condemning Nieh and others as "renegades," "anti-Party elements," "ambitious characters," and "underlings of the Teng T'o black gang" who were trying to "undermine the movement." They proclaimed that Lu P'ing's committee was a "Marxist-Leninist Party Committee," and added, "To oppose the school's Party organ is to oppose the Party Central Committee and to oppose Lu P'ing is to oppose the Party."[13] "By 6:00 P.M.," Nieh told Anna Louise Strong, "our poster was covered by many posters abusing us. By seven we were 'besieged' (that is, encircled in small groups and yelled at) and physically struck."

That evening, teachers and students from the philosophy department held a mass meeting. As they were finishing, a group of people "headed by Lu P'ing" entered and "demanded to 'interrogate' Nieh Yuan-tzu." Sun Yueh-ts'ai, a research assistant in philosophy, reports that this group then mounted the rostrum in the dining hall, questioned Nieh Yuan-tzu, and accused her of various "crimes." They accused the leftists of

11. Interview with Jean-François Billeter by Ruth Padrum, "Chine: De la révolte des étudiants à la révolution culturelle," in Croissance des Jeunes Nations, Dossier du Mois, July-August 1968, pp. 19-26, and interview with Marianne Bastid.
12. NCNA (by a staff correspondent), June 1, 1967.
13. "Revolutionary Storm at Peking University," NCNA, June 5, 1966.

wanting to shift the struggle away from the "'Three-Family Village" of Teng T'o, Wu Han, and Liao Mo-sha. Some people praised these speeches. Sun decided to intervene.

Seeing that some fellow students were deceived, I went up to the rostrum and spoke. I said that these people had entered the classroom and disturbed the order and tried to wreck the meeting, and that we did not intend to change the target of struggle. I said that by exposing the Party Committee we could better strike at the "Three-Family Village" black gang. Before I could continue, they cursed and shouted at me and pushed me off the platform. Some held up their fists and wanted to hit me. (They were stopped by the comrades who secretly supported me.) Some shouted: "Don't let him go. Take him to the University guards!"

Later, these people again took me to the platform and asked me to finish my speech. I said that we must not create a split among the students, and that I believed that 99 percent of the students (I now admit my estimate was too high) wanted to safeguard the Party Central Committee and the thought of Mao Tse-tung and to struggle against the "Three-Family Village" black gang.

After I said this, there were shouts of "rubbish!" below the platform. Then I was again pushed off the platform.

Marianne Bastid says she walked into the dining hall at about this point and some people began dragging Sun outside. They told Sun they would argue the matter out with him.

So they inquisitioned me, heaping questions on me. They cursed me and called me a "running dog of Teng T'o," "a rightist," "anti-Party element," etc. Finally, I was violently pushed down from the high ground [outside the dining hall] by these people.

At this time, the Party Committee sent a man to the scene. The people who had manhandled me pulled me up before him, and I stated my views. With a cold expression, he did not say anything except to ask me to go back. But these people still were not willing to let go of me. They took me to the office of the [Youth] League Committee and wanted to continue to "argue" with me.

Thus I was illegally and brutally maltreated and persecuted by them for more than two hours.[14]

14. Sun Yueh-ts'ai, "I Denounce This Illegal and Brutal Act," *Jen-min Jih-pao* (*People's Daily*), June 5, 1966.

After Sun had been dragged out of the dining hall, Marianne Bastid asked a Chinese student studying in the French department how she felt about the controversy. She replied, in French, that Lu P'ing was probably right. But two other girls standing nearby said that it was not just "probable" but definite that Lu P'ing was correct.[15]

It appears that that evening almost everyone, with the exception of a small group of leftist students and teaching fellows, was arguing, at least publicly, that Lu P'ing was right. But passions were clearly aroused on both sides. "All through the night people argued, put up posters, and engaged in fighting that broke spectacles, watches, and fountain pens."[16]

The following week seems to have been generally calm on the surface, although the most active rebels experienced a "reign of terror." Nieh Yuan-tzu told Anna Louise Strong: "I couldn't go out of doors without being grabbed, my clothing pulled, and being yelled at as 'chief Rightist.'" However, students continued to discuss Nieh's poster in small groups, and Billeter says many students continued to oppose Lu P'ing, not only because this might permit them to discuss "Hai Jui" and the underlying political questions freely, but also because it might lead to a solution to the many outstanding problems within the university itself. Some of these students, he says, took the text of the May 25 poster to the Central People's Radio station. Be that as it may, "On the evening of June 1, Chairman Mao telephoned Comrade K'ang Sheng [now a member of the Standing Committee] demanding that the wall poster written by Nieh Yuan-tzu and six other comrades be broadcast and published at once."[17] Later, in his own poster "Bombard the Headquarters," Mao described this as "China's first Marxist-Leninist big-character poster," no doubt recalling the liberal posters at Peita during the Hundred Flowers period.

15. Interview with Marianne Bastid.
16. Nieh Yuan-tzu in her interview with Anna Louise Strong.
17. "Down With Liu Shao-ch'i" (a chronical of events in Liu's life from 1899 to 1967 reprinted by the Chingkangshan Fighting Corps of the Fourth Hospital, Peking, dated May 1967), *Current Background*, No. 834.

At eight o'clock the same evening (June 1) Peita students were called to a meeting at which the text was broadcast, followed by a favorable commentary. Nieh Yuan-tzu then spoke to a large gathering, and "everyone" immediately began siding with the rebels against Lu P'ing and his close associates. Or almost everyone:

> That night, a responsible member of the "General Office of the Party Committee for Directing the Cultural Revolution" hurriedly entered the big mess hall to threaten teachers and students who were listening to the broadcast "not to believe blindly" in the broadcast items. Someone even rabidly shouted at the mess hall, saying that "within three hours the arrogant airs of the Central People's Radio will be put out."[18]

They weren't, however, and cymbals and gongs resounded throughout the night. The following day, there were parades of university and secondary school students, cadres, workers, and even some suburban peasants who came to bring posters and make speeches supporting the revolutionaries of Peita.[19] Shortly after midnight, Wu Te, the second secretary of a newly reorganized Peking Municipal Committee, arrived on the campus to announce that P'eng Chen had been dismissed and that the new Committee had decided to dismiss Lu P'ing and P'eng P'ei-yun from all their posts.[20]

By all accounts, this decision led to a wild outburst of enthusiasm in the days that followed. While there was probably a certain amount of opportunism in the changed attitudes of a few students, most appear to have been greatly relieved by the collapse of Lu P'ing's administration. Political and social activity had been strictly supervised under the old order, and the University Party apparatus had established a regime under which students were expected to report any of their fellow students' rebellious thoughts to higher authority or face the prospect of having a black mark placed in their permanent records. At times students appear to have been afraid to enter

18. NCNA, June 5, 1966.
19. Interview with Marianne Bastid.
20. NCNA, June 5, 1966.

into friendships and talk openly about their thoughts and feelings. This may help account for the tension and the almost desperate violence directed against the rebel students before it became clear that Lu P'ing had lost his powers of reprisal. The new mood was captured by even so skeptical an observer as the local Reuters correspondent:

> Students talked in excited groups and chanted slogans under trees and buildings draped with colored paper streamers. The atmosphere seemed festive rather than tense. . . .
> Columns of demonstrators paraded around the wall surrounding the University grounds. Students at dormitory windows shouted slogans in unison and sang revolutionary songs.[21]

Criticism of Lu P'ing by the politically most active students centered on his educational policies. Their posters, which Marianne Bastid recalls as having been generally well reasoned and eloquent, denounced Lu for opposing many aspects of the Educational Revolution and discriminating against the students from worker and peasant families. But since over 100,000 sheets of wall-newspapers were posted during that first week of June, many were naturally of considerably lower analytic quality. Some students attacked the former president's personal life, partly on the basis of a raid on his house when some of his personal papers had been seized. He was criticized for the number of beds he owned and the fact that his daughter had taken an expensive holiday.[22] A number of other Party officials and professors, especially those who had adopted "lordly airs" toward the poorer students, were criticized at mass meetings. They were then told to relieve the regular gardeners and pick weeds in the hot June sun.

Under the auspices of the new Municipal Committee, more workers and peasants from neighboring areas came to the campus to demonstrate support. Carrying banners and posters, they marched in to the beat of drums and the clash of cymbals. Students met them with enthusiastic greetings, and registered

21. Reuters, Peking, June 5, 1966; *New York Times,* June 6.
22. Interview with Marianne Bastid.

them at special tables. Wanting to explain why they had attacked Lu P'ing, the students began to set up makeshift rostrums in Hyde Park fashion, and organized speakers.

Many of the students at first seemed to lack a theoretical basis for their attacks on Lu P'ing, and they acted largely in the context of their somewhat mechanical "official lives." But in the days that followed a change began to occur. Their "official" political lives gradually began to become integrated with their private lives as, lacking theoretical notions, they found they had to talk in very personal terms about their lives under the old administration. Students described their feelings of oppression and intimidation. Some of the girls' speeches were like "Greek tragedies": swept up by their emotions, crying and tearing out their hair, they related how miserable they had been.[23]

Among the most indignant speakers were some of the nearly six thousand students, teachers, and other workers who had been sent to the countryside or to factories the previous fall and who had been permitted to return by decision of the new Municipal Committee.[24] Jean-François Billeter recalls having seen many of them arriving in the middle of the night, worn out from long trips, furious at what they now felt had been deception on the part of the old university authorities, but filled with revolutionary ideas from their work at the grass-roots level.

During these days, Peking University was transformed. Students who had been afraid to talk to one another began to express their deep feelings; they began to think about their education, the quality of their lives, and the forces that controlled them. A new sense of student solidarity began to grow.

----

23. *Ibid.*
24. NCNA, June 5, 1966.

4

Summer 1966:
New Peking University

The period of uninterrupted speech-making and poster-pasting during which students spoke and wrote as they pleased lasted about a week. Beginning on or around June 7, members of a work team sent by the new Municipal Committee began to take an active role in "leadership over the great proletarian revolution in Peking University."[1] The work team, headed by Chang Ch'eng-hsien, had been organized about June 3 and arrived at Peita on June 4, to assist, it was announced, in the reorganization of the University Party Committee. The team appears to have been welcomed on its arrival, especially because the work team which had been active at Peita during the Socialist Education movement the year before had sided with the critics of the old administration. But it soon became clear that this team's role would be quite different in the new circumstances created by the active student rebellion.

By June 12, the demonstrations had stopped and the work team locked the gates of the University. To "calm" the most enthusiastic activists, members of the team assigned them such chores as scraping the posters off the walls.[2] No one was allowed to enter the University grounds without showing identification. Students were told to stop their speech-making. Control over their growing movement was wrested from the stu-

---

1. NCNA, June 8, 1966; *Jen-min Jih-pao* (*People's Daily*), June 9.
2. Interview with Marianne Bastid.

dents, and the work team began to assume the role of the previous school administration.

Considerable mystery surrounds the ensuing period of work-team domination at Peita. Since 1966, Red Guards have written many accounts of work-team activity during this period in their unofficial newspapers, magazines, and pamphlets, but Peita has received less national attention than some of the other Peking schools. Reports we have read of an incident which occurred on June 18 lack detail, but it appears to have had serious consequences.

One of the work team's first acts, it is said, was to send Lu P'ing and other high officials off the campus, "ostensibly to have them write their self-criticisms, but really to shield them from the struggle meetings."[3] The students were told that if they wished to confront these officials, they "must first have a plan, get organized, and get sanction from the work team."

Feeling themselves protected by the work team, the black-liners—that is, those who were conscious counter-revolutionaries—dared to jibe at the students: "Come on, why don't you struggle with me?" Indeed, in all the fifty-six days they spent at Peita, the work team never once organized a struggle meeting against the monsters.[4]

But on June 18, in defiance of the work team, Lu P'ing and some others were brought before a struggle meeting. "There, after strong criticism, they were condemned."[5] There was probably some violence. The work team labeled the affair a counter-revolutionary act, and many participants who were Party or Youth League members were expelled from those organizations. All participants were required to make self-criticism, some as many as five times. Less radical students were organized to struggle against the rebel students. As the conflict grew, the campus was sealed off still more tightly, inter-faculty exchanges on the campus itself were prevented, and students who wanted to visit their homes had to get a permit from the work team.

---

3. "How It All Started," pp. 26-27.
4. *Ibid.*
5. *Ibid.*

Students who appealed to the spirit of Mao Tse-tung's famous "Report on an Investigation of the Peasant Movement in Hunan," written in March 1927, were told by work team members that it was "out of date."[6]

Mao's "Report" includes this passage:

People swarm into the houses of local tyrants and evil gentry who are against the peasant association, slaughter their pigs and consume their grain. They even loll for a minute or two on the ivory-inlaid beds belonging to the young ladies. . . . This is what some people call "going too far," or "exceeding the proper limits in righting a wrong," or "really too much." Such talk may seem plausible, but in fact it is wrong. . . . The most violent revolts and the most serious disorders have invariably occurred in places where the local tyrants, evil gentry, and lawless landlords perpetrated the worst outrages. The peasants are clear-sighted. Who is bad and who is not, who is the worst and who is not quite so vicious, who deserves severe punishment and who deserves to be let off lightly—the peasants keep clear accounts, and very seldom has the punishment exceeded the crime. Secondly, a revolution is not a dinner party, or writing an essay, or painting a picture, or doing embroidery; it cannot be so refined, so leisurely and gentle, so temperate, kind, courteous, restrained and magnanimous.[7]

The work team also seems to have attempted to carry out "rectification" of other students, officials, and professors, but since it was made up of outsiders, the decisions on who was selected for criticism were often arbitrary. Marianne Bastid cited one example of a woman professor who appears to have been singled out simply because she held a position of authority in the Party branch committee of the Language Department. When one of her students was called upon by the work team to lead a session of criticism against her, the student refused. She argued that she had no grounds for criticizing her professor, and described her as a good Communist and a person she trusted. The work team thereupon organized a struggle meeting

6. *Ibid.*
7. *Selected Works of Mao Tse-tung,* Vol. I (Peking: Foreign Languages Press, 1965), p. 28.

at which this student was severely criticized for refusing to lead the rectification of her professor; that evening the girl wept quietly in her room.[8]

Students increasingly began to criticize the work team for its actions. But instead of becoming self-critical, the team, which was receiving the direct support of Liu Shao-ch'i, China's head of state and at this time the highest-ranking member of the Central Committee in charge of routine work, branded its critics "counter-revolutionaries" and "rightists."[9] Thus the work team period became known among the students as the "fifty days of white terror."

However, on July 12, five students in geophysics (some sources say zoology) finally spearheaded a revolt by putting up a big-character poster denouncing the work team.[10] The work team in turn accused the students of trying to usurp their leadership, but Nieh Yuan-tzu went into action and made a speech on July 19 which initiated a big debate among students and staff over the June 18 incident. "This meeting came to the conclusion that it was entirely correct to have carried out the struggle meeting against Lu P'ing."[11] Students also accused members of the work team of having "Kuomintang-like attitudes," and failing to place any faith in the judgment of the students.[12]

The work team continued to hold struggle sessions against its critics and forced them to wear dunce caps. It still took considerable courage to side with the rebels. Before joining

---

8. Interview.
9. Liu's wife, Wang Kuang-mei, was even more directly involved. According to the pamphlet, "Down With Liu Shao-ch'i," cited earlier: "On June 19, Liu Shao-ch'i sent Wang Kuang-mei to Tsinghua [University] to carry out activity. On June 21, Wang Kuang-mei formally laid her hand on the great proletarian Cultural Revolution at Tsinghua. She branded more than 800 revolutionary teachers and students represented by Comrade K'uai Ta-fu as 'counter-revolutionaries,' 'pseudo-leftists but genuine rightists,' and spread white terror that brought about the death of one person and caused many persons to commit suicide."
10. Interview with Nieh Yuan-tzu by NCNA, June 2, 1967.
11. "How It All Started," p. 28.
12. Interview with Marianne Bastid.

the Left, one student thought to himself, "But if I should fail in the struggle, would that affect my Party membership application, the assignment of work to me after graduation, my personal future, and so on? A series of personal considerations caught me in a well of worries. . . ."[13] But more and more students were won over. It became harder and harder for the work team to isolate the Left, even though students were told that they could expiate their own previous sins by attacking the biggest "troublemakers." Only a few students, mostly the sons and daughters of high-ranking officials—perhaps foreseeing that their parents would be criticized most severely in the course of the movement ahead—continued to side with the work team long after the latter had been dismissed. (These students were later to form such conservative "Red Guard" organizations as the United Action Committee and the Crimson Banner Guards.) The tide was turning against the work teams and their high-placed supporters.

On July 18, Mao returned to Peking from Shanghai, where he had been since November, and immediately criticized the conduct of the work teams.[14] On July 22, Chiang Ch'ing, Mao's wife and a member of the new Cultural Revolution Group which had been set up in May to replace the group under P'eng Chen, together with Ch'en Po-ta and K'ang Sheng, also members of the new group, began a series of visits to the Peita campus. (K'ang Sheng and Ch'en Po-ta are now two of the five most powerful men in China.) They devoted most of the first day to reading posters. The following day, Ch'en Po-ta had this to say:

We have come as pupils to learn from you, and study how you debate. We are not your teachers. Our minds are just like a white blank. We must first learn from you before we can teach you. . . . In your big debate, you must also teach and learn from each other. . . . We must always set out the facts and abide by reasoning. I hope that you will "draw strength" from Chairman Mao's teaching concerning the method of conducting study and

---

13. *Jen-min Jih-pao* (*People's Daily*), December 20, 1966.
14. "Down With Liu Shao-ch'i."

research work, so that we may make a greater success of the great Cultural Revolution. Now I am going to make a pupil of myself.[15]

On July 25, K'ang Sheng gave this summation of the group's investigations:

I've heard that you comrades hold different opinions on certain problems. This is a very good, normal, and healthy phenomenon. Truth can be made clearer through contention. For instance, regarding the "June 18" event, some said that it was revolutionary while others regarded it as counter-revolutionary. Still others considered that it was neither revolutionary nor counter-revolutionary. . . . How is the work team? It is said that opinions differ. Some think that it is good. Others say that it has made some mistakes. Some even say that it is wrong in line or that it has taken the wrong line.

Open your mind and speak out. You may say what you want, free from misgivings. . . .

Neither we, nor the work team, but you are the masters of the great Cultural Revolution. This is precisely the important point which Chairman Mao has sent us to tell you in the first place.[16]

The next day (July 26), the group felt it was able to draw some preliminary conclusions. K'ang Sheng announced the group's opinion on Chang Ch'eng-hsien's work team, saying that it had made two big mistakes. First, it had not encouraged the active participation of the revolutionary students and teachers of the whole University in carrying out the Cultural Revolution. Second, no effort had been made to organize a new representative organ of power, "and work in each department is also under the 'monopoly' of the work team. . . . The masses are not boldly aroused, trusted, or relied upon in the real sense. Therefore, Chang Ch'eng-hsien has committed grave mistakes in line, in thought, and in organizational work." Ch'en Po-ta offered the group's recommendations to the students, faculty, and staff at Peita:

15. "Excerpts from Talks at Peking University by Leaders of the Cultural Revolution Group under the CCP Central Committee," acquired by the U. S. Consulate General, Hong Kong, *Current Background*, No. 830.
16. *Ibid.*

I recommend, first, that the work team headed by Chang Ch'eng-hsien be dissolved, and second, that leading groups for the Cultural Revolution be formed in Peking University, and that a Cultural Revolution Committee or a Cultural Revolution representative conference be organized for the whole university.... The representatives of these organizations should not be appointed by anybody but should be elected by the masses. There should be plenty of time for preparing the list of candidates from among the masses. . . . No haste is called for. The list thus prepared should be made public, and everybody should vote by ballot. These representatives are your service personnel; they should serve you and should not ride on your back. . . . You must pay attention to the public's being broadly represented in elections, and you must be able to hear different kinds of opinion. The teachers and office workers should have their own representatives. These representatives are not elected for life. They may be removed any time they are found to be incompetent. The masses may remove them and replace them with other persons through re-election. You may discuss this recommendation.[17]

The work team was disbanded the same day, and the suggestions for a system of representative committees modeled on the principles of the Paris Commune of 1871 are reported to have been met with enormous enthusiasm. The next day the students decided to organize their own Cultural Revolution Committee, and a preparatory committee was formed to lay the groundwork.[18]

Once the work team was discredited, the Peking Municipal Committee formally apologized to the rebels and reinstated those who had been expelled for attacking the work team. The work team was instructed to destroy the records it had compiled against the students and to return any "confessions." It was further stipulated that none of this material could be made public. Exuberant at their victory, the students raised banners inscribed "Hsin Peita"—New Peking University—over the main entrance-way of the school.

Students were now participating in making their own political decisions, and they found the process exhilarating. One

17. *Ibid.*
18. "How It All Started," p. 28.

student told Marianne Bastid: "Now that we dare to speak, dare to act, it's wonderful! We've never felt like this before." Thousands of posters inscribed with quotations from Mao Tse-tung were pasted-up throughout the campus. Posters covered the walls of the corridors and classrooms; students even mounted quotations from Mao over their beds. The campus was thrown into a state of round-the-clock meetings, large and small, where students and teachers discussed what to do next, the strategy of the Cultural Revolution, and how they should change the educational system. They carried on long theoretical discussions interspersed with fiery speeches on how best to apply the teachings of Marx, Lenin, and Mao to the concrete problems facing China. Study-groups for reading and discussing Mao's writings were formed or revived.[19]

Rebel students delivered strong critiques of the old educational system, saying that it worked to inculcate a bourgeois and revisionist mentality. They argued that because it one-sidedly stressed academic achievement and high professional standards, students were being trained to be more concerned about their individual advancement than about the public good, and were receiving mainly a book-knowledge which was often divorced from Chinese reality. Because the former administration had greatly reduced student involvement in work-projects in the factories and communes, they felt they were inadequately prepared to help solve the practical problems of China's socialist development. They feared they would develop elitist, technocratic attitudes, and that a new privileged stratum would develop as it had in the Soviet Union. Many Peita students therefore voiced support for some general proposals for change that had been advanced in June by a group of students at China People's University.[20]

The proposals of the People's University students were these:

(1) As soon as the great Cultural Revolution ends, all those students who have done at least two years in the arts

---

19. Interview with Marianne Bastid.
20. Bastid interview and sources in the Chinese press.

faculties will be graduated ahead of time and assigned to take part in the three great revolutionary movements of class struggle, the struggle for production, and scientific experimentation, and will for a long time unreservedly integrate themselves with the workers, peasants, and soldiers.

(2) The arts faculties must use Mao Tse-tung's works as teaching material and take class struggle as the subject of profound study.

(3) From now on the arts faculties should change their course of study to one, two, or three years, in accordance with Chairman Mao's instructions and the requirements of the country. In addition, a certain amount of time each year should be devoted to taking part in factory or farm work, military drill, and class struggle in society.

(4) In teaching methods, the stress should be on self-education and discussion. Teachers should give adequate tutoring, practice the democratic method of teaching, follow the mass line, and resolutely abolish the cramming method of teaching.

(5) From now on the colleges should enroll new students from among young people who have tempered themselves in the three great revolutionary movements, whose ideology is progressive, and who have reached a certain educational level, and not necessarily just from those who have been through senior middle school. This will enable great numbers of outstanding workers, former poor and lower-middle peasants, and demobilized army men to be admitted to college.[21]

Professor C. H. G. Oldham, who is one of the best-known foreign students of Chinese science and who has contributed articles on China to the *Bulletin of the Atomic Scientists* both before and since the Cultural Revolution began, argues that the new revolutionary educational policies are probably a good thing for China's development. He suggests that if Liu Shaoch'i and his supporters had been victorious, there might have

---

21. "Proposals to the Party Central Committee and Chairman Mao Concerning the Introduction of a Completely New Academic System of Arts Faculties in Universities," June 22, 1966. Published in the *People's Daily* of July 12.

been a greater amount of advanced scientific research in the short run, but less attention would have been paid to bringing the scientific revolution to the peasants. By the year 2000, he feels, China will have a population of some 1,300 million, most with some education in science, and the manpower-resource base for recruiting talent for basic research will be enormous.[22]

Preparations for election of the new Cultural Revolution Committee continued in August, and the Peita Preparatory Committee held a congress from August 30 to September 12. Following this, a Cultural Revolution Committee of forty-five members and eight alternates was elected by the entire student body and staff. The Committee in turn chose a standing committee of fifteen, led by Nieh Yuan-tzu.[23] Then, during the fall and winter, a congress of Red Guards from all of Peking's colleges and universities was gradually organized. Nieh Yuan-tzu played an active role in this. Anna Louise Strong remarks: "It was not easy to bring together into one unified organization the thousands of Red Guard groups which had sprung up spontaneously, always several and sometimes a hundred groups in one university and many of them fighting one another."[24] About twenty of the largest organizations held a preliminary conference, which set up a "core group" to call a congress; this "core" was later elected a standing committee for all Peking.[25]

The Congress of Red Guards of Universities and Colleges in Peking was finally convened in late February 1967, and more than 10,000 representatives were present at the inaugural meeting.[26] On March 19, 2,500 representatives of poor and

---

22. "Science for the Masses?" *Far Eastern Economic Review* (Hong Kong), May 12-18, 1968, pp. 353-355. The article was originally read at an April 1968 Seminar on Contemporary China at the University of Guelph, Ontario.
23. "How It All Started," pp. 29-30.
24. "Cultural Revolution at Beida," *Progressive Labor,* Vol. 6, No. 2. (November-December 1967), p. 77.
25. *Ibid.*
26. *Peking Review,* March 10, 1967.

lower-middle peasants from thirteen suburban counties and districts set up a congress, and this was followed on March 22 by a congress of revolutionary workers and staff in Peking industry and mining. Red Guards from Peking secondary schools set up their own congress on March 25. Representatives of these four organizations hold about four-fifths of the seats in the Peking Revolutionary Committee established on April 20, 1967, to replace the Peking Municipal Party Committee.

Nieh Yuan-tzu became a vice chairman of the Peking Committee, and in April 1969 she was elected one of the 109 alternate members of the Ninth Central Committee of the Communist Party. In 1967, she discussed the defects of the old system with Anna Louise Strong, and gave her opinion as to how matters had been improved:

In 1949, when we set up the People's Republic, we seized power only at the top. We retained much of the old apparatus in government and in the economy. Such a seizure could not guarantee us against revisionism or "peaceful evolution" to capitalism.

In the post-Liberation years three things came together: the elements of the old apparatus, the ideology of the remaining bourgeoisie, and revisionism. The combination produced a greatly swollen bureaucratic apparatus increasingly divorced from the people. . . .

That bureaucratic structure has now been smashed by the Cultural Revolution, which was a rising of the masses against all bourgeois survivals and tendencies.

Nieh added that she believed there were essentially three reasons why the new organs of power were a great improvement. First, representatives came mostly from the ranks of the rebels. Second, they maintained close contact with those who had chosen them: "When you see a representative reporting to his factory or rural commune, with all his fellow workers discussing his policies, you see that the connection of the working class with the Peking Revolutionary Committee's activities is very direct." Finally, the representatives continue to work in the shops, on the farms, or in schools, and do not receive salaries as officials. Miss Strong asked Nieh whether she thought this was practical: "If they work in factories, have they time to run city affairs?"

Nieh replied that this is indeed a serious problem and is being considered very seriously. Many suggestions have been made to keep the government under the continuous supervision and direction of the people. Basically it is hoped to develop a widening mass participation in state affairs such as Marx and Lenin foresaw as the prerequisite for communist society. The "revolutionary masses" are seizing power not only through their representatives in the Peking Revolutionary Committee, but also directly, in their factories, communes, or institutions, through the "revolutionary rebels" within.[27]

To understand fully the forces which brought about all these changes, it is necessary to return to the late spring and early summer of 1966. The secondary-school Red Guards—to become one of the mightiest revolutionary forces—appeared at this time. The first Red Guards were organized at the middle school attached to Tsinghua University in Peking. In an interview with Japanese correspondents who visited their school on October 10, 1966, this is how they described themselves:

We first formed our organization on May 29, and named it the Red Guards. Since the Liberation, this school has always been controlled by bourgeois people, and for this reason, even when we tried to study Mao Tse-tung's thought and carry out the great Cultural Revolution, joining hands with the workers, peasants, and soldiers, we were obstructed by Principal Wang Pang-ju, who held power. The organization was formed when our anger exploded at this, and it was formed voluntarily. The organization consisted of about forty members. . . . Today, 265 out of the 1,300 students at this school are members.[28]

---

27. "Cultural Revolution at Beida," p. 78.
28. *Nihon Keizai (Japan Economic News)*, October 12, 1966. The students added: "As a result, Principal Wang has been separated from his work as principal since June, and together with eight other reactionary teachers, he is now engaging in reform through labor, coming to school every day and cleaning the school or raising vegetables in the backyard.

"There are sixteen Red Guards among the 150 teachers and staff. Eighty percent of the student Red Guards here come from the five Red classes [poor and lower-middle peasants, workers, revolutionary leaders, and families of revolutionary heroes].

The authors of "How It All Started" say that secondary-school rebels began to write many big-character posters criticizing the work teams after the June 18 incident at Peita. In late July, some of these students sent two of their attacks on the old order to Mao Tse-tung, who immediately replied:

I have received the two big-character posters which you mailed to me on July 28, and also the letter which you transmitted to me with the request that I reply to it.

Your two big-character posters written on June 24 and July 4 respectively express indignation against and denunciation of the landlord class, the bourgeoisie, imperialism, and revisionism as well as their jackals who exploit and oppose the workers, peasants, revolutionary intellectuals, and revolutionary groups and parties. You show that rebellion against reactionaries is justified.

I hereby give you my enthusiastic support. . . .

Here I must say that my revolutionary comrades-in-arms and I adopt the same revolutionary attitude: that whether in Peking or in other parts of the country or in the course of the Cultural Revolution, all those who take the same attitude as you do shall have our enthusiastic support.

Besides, while we support you, we also ask you to turn your attention to uniting with all those who can be united with. As for those who have made serious mistakes, after their mistakes have been pointed out to them, they too must be given a chance to work, to correct their mistakes, and to start life anew.

Marx said that the proletariat must liberate not only itself but all mankind. If it is unable to liberate all mankind, then the proletariat too will not achieve ultimate self-liberation. I would urge you comrades to heed this truth.

Mao Tse-tung
August 1, 1966[29]

The same day, August 1, the eleventh plenary session of the Eighth Central Committee was convened. Mao put up his own big-character poster, entitled "Bombard the Headquarters!", at the meeting of August 5. In it, he called on the representatives to read the original May 24 Peita poster again, and stated that in the previous fifty days "some leading comrades from the central down to the local levels" had "enforced a bourgeois dictatorship. . . . They have stood facts on their head

---

29. "Chairman Mao's Letter to Us," *Hung-wei-ping Pao* (*The Red Guard Newspaper*), August 14, 1968.

and juggled black and white, encircled and suppressed revolutionaries, stifled opinions differing from their own, imposed a White terror, and felt very pleased with themselves." He concluded by inquiring, "Shouldn't this prompt one to deep thought?" Mao's poster encouraged a slight majority to agree to issuing the sixteen-point "Decision of the Central Committee of the Chinese Communist Party Concerning the Great Proletarian Cultural Revolution" on August 8. This document analyzed the new stage of the revolution and listed its main objectives and the means of carrying them out.

According to Marianne Bastid, enthusiasm at Peking University now reached its height. People descended on the campus from everywhere—by bus, in trucks, on bicycles, or on foot, with no special organization, as there had been in June, and no letters of introduction—and made their way through a labyrinth of sandwich and lemonade stands. By the middle of the month, Red Guards were everywhere, especially after their reception at The Gate of Heavenly Peace, where Mao himself accepted one of their armbands. Before August 23, most of the Red Guards had been secondary-school students, but by the beginning of September the spectrum had broadened to include people from six to well over thirty. The university students who joined the movement in these weeks probably helped to channel some of the passion which had led to excesses on the part of a few of the younger rebels.

Peita students not only acted as hosts to some seven million visitors between the end of July and October 1966; they also began making their own visits. Groups traveled to other university centers throughout China, and later went in large numbers to work in factories and communes in order to exchange experience with citizens in all walks of life. They revived the traditions of the Peking students of 1919 and 1935 and fading memories of the great Long March. Like the students during the Hundred Flowers campaign, they spoke their minds, but now they started to criticize their own privileges; and they began to make their way down a long, winding path to unite with China's workers and peasants.

Appendix

The following articles are taken from the Peking Red Guard paper Spring Thunder, *of April 13, 1967. The paper is published by the capital's "August 1" school, one of the elite schools for children of high-ranking Peking Party officials. The articles are important because they began the movement for abolishing these elite schools; they are also vivid examples of Red Guard journalism.*

ON COLLECTIVE BOARDING SCHOOLS

FOR CHILDREN OF CADRES

*"The spring thunder resounds through the skies;
the east wind sweeps across the great earth."*

The torrent of the Great Proletarian Cultural Revolution is attacking all the superstructures which are not adaptable to the foundation of our socialist economy.

All the old educational systems are in a state of great confusion and collapse.

Doomsday has come for the bourgeois educational line which is represented by Liu Shao-ch'i, Teng Hsiao-p'ing, and Lu Ting-i!

The war drum is beaten aloud for thoroughly liquidating and smashing to pieces the revisionist system of collective boarding schools for children of cadres!

1

The collective boarding schools for children of cadres were first introduced in the warring years before the Liberation. They had their glorious history in the past.

In those years of civil war, the broad masses of fighters and cadres were risking their lives to fight for the liberation of the whole nation all over the country. Furthermore, they were paid in kind. So that their children could be looked after and educated, it was necessary to establish a number of collective boarding schools for the children of cadres. At that time, these schools were situated in mountain villages and the students lived through hardships along with the broad masses of the local people. They had developed our glorious tradition of fighting amid great hardships and trained themselves to be successors to our revolutionary cause.

In the period immediately after the liberation of the whole country, the cadres were frequently transferred, and the system of paying cadres in kind was not entirely altered: it was permissible to continue for a certain period these collective boarding schools for the children of cadres. However, under the domination of a handful of persons in the Party in authority taking the capitalist road, the nature of these schools has gradually changed. Schools have undertaken large-scale construction projects, built splendid dormitories, and allowed the children of cadres to live a very comfortable life in their "paradise of another world." They have been cut off completely from their contact with the masses of workers and peasants. The glorious tradition of fighting among hardships has been given up. This handful of bad eggs has openly opposed the educational policy of Chairman Mao, energetically peddled the black goods of revisionist education, and led these collective boarding schools for children of cadres gradually onto the road of "schools for aristocratic children" of the British and Soviet types.

The CCP Central Committee and Chairman Mao very quickly realized the seriousness of the problem concerning the collective boarding schools for children of the cadres, and have issued many orders and instructions to prevent these schools from enjoying any special privileges. Furthermore, there is no need for these schools to continue to exist. Following the development of our economic and cultural construction, a huge network of schools which will meet the educational requirements of the children of cadres already covers the whole country. The cadres of all levels have also generally carried on their work steadily. Particularly since July 1955, they have all been paid wages. It is, therefore, unreasonable for the state to continue to appropriate large sums of money to run schools for the children of the cadres.

Consequently, in 1955 the Party Central Committee issued instructions to abolish gradually the schools for children of cadres.

However, under the domination of a handful of persons in the Party in authority taking the capitalist road, not only have the collective boarding schools for children of cadres not been abolished, but their number has rapidly increased. According to statistics, at present two-thirds of the thirty-odd collective boarding schools for children of cadres in Peking were established after 1955.

In this way, schools which fostered revolutionary successors in former years have gradually transformed themselves into hotbeds for nurturing the seeds of revisionism. The big families of revolution which were full of revolutionary vitality in former years have gradually taken black positions against Mao Tsetung's thought. Those collective boarding schools for children of cadres which were set up after 1955 have, from the first day of their founding, slid toward the abyss of "peaceful evolution."

2

That the collective boarding schools for children of cadres have existed for too long a time and continuously increased in number is a reflection of the struggle between the two classes, and between the two roads and two ideologies [of capitalism and socialism] over more than ten years in our country.

Chairman Mao has said:

In China, although in the main socialist transformation has been completed with respect to the system of ownership and although the large-scale and turbulent class struggles of the masses characteristic of the previous revolutionary periods have in the main come to an end, there are still remnants of the overthrown landlord and comprador classes, there is still a bourgeoisie, and the remolding of the petty bourgeoisie has only just started. The class struggle is by no means over. The class struggle between the proletariat and the bourgeoisie, the class struggle between the different political forces, and the class struggle in the ideological field between the proletariat and the bourgeoisie will continue to be long and tortuous and at times will even become very acute. The proletariat seeks to transform the world according to its own world outlook, and so does the bourgeoisie. In this respect, the question of which will win out, socialism or capitalism, is still not really settled.

To carry out their scheme for "peaceful evolution" in China, the handful of persons in the Party in authority taking the capitalist road have all the time been vying with the proletariat in all fields. The educational front has always been one of the foci of their violent struggles with the proletariat.

Over many years, Liu Shao-ch'i, Teng Hsiao-p'ing, and Lu Ting-i have utilized powers which they usurped to promote energetically in the domain of education a bourgeois educational line in opposition to Chairman Mao's revolutionary line, and they have taken the frontline of education as a position for fostering their successors.

The persons in the Party in authority taking the capitalist road have long treated the collective boarding schools for children of cadres as their particular treasure, and have taken them as a hotbed for cultivating the seeds of revisionism. The top person in authority taking the capitalist road in our country, Liu Shao-ch'i, has personally spread poison among the teachers of the Yü-ying Primary School and trumpeted the "superiority" of the collective boarding schools for children of the cadres. Yang Shang-kun, the anti-Party and anti-socialist element, has even personally scrutinized the construction plan for the site of the Yü-ying Primary School and, furthermore, shamelessly claimed that "the Yü-ying Primary School is the cherished child of the Party Committee for Organs Directly Attached to the Central Party Committee." Liu Jen, the counter-revolutionary revisionist element of the former CCP Peking Municipal Committee, has also personally taken the responsibility of running the Peking Primary School and declared openly that "schools of this category have turned out dragon seeds"!

In short, the reason why those persons in the Party in authority taking the capitalist road have so stubbornly maintained and set up increasing numbers of the privileged collective boarding schools for children of the cadres is that they are trying to win over the younger generation from the proletariat, to build up bases for educating their own successors, and to restore capitalism in China.

Many of our cadres are able to follow the teachings of Chairman Mao, make strict demands on themselves, and educate their own children with Mao Tse-tung's thought. Among them, some have already seen the dangers of the collective boarding schools for children of the cadres and have never allowed their children to enter these schools. Though a number of cadres wanted to educate their children, they did not see clearly the nature of these schools and blindly sent their children to them. Consequently, they have been greatly disappointed.

Besides, we also have to see that during the whole period of socialism, classes and class struggles will exist for a long time. The exploiting class will try by any and every means to spread through various channels of the society the poisons of capitalism, feudalism, and revisionism in order to corrode our revolutionary rank and file. Chairman Mao has said: "It is possible that there are a number of Communists who have never been conquered by enemies holding guns and are worthy of the name hero before these enemies. However, they cannot withstand the attacks of people using sugar-coated bullets. They will be defeated by these sugar-coated bullets." Truly, there are some cadres who have, for a long time and in peaceful circumstances, lived in special political and economic positions. They have relaxed their vigilance and allowed the bourgeois ideology and the force of habit in the society to corrode their own souls in different degrees. They have not treated their own children and the children of the broad workers and peasants on an equal basis, but have considered that theirs should be higher than others and should enjoy special privileges. They refuse to allow their own children to develop the glorious tradition of the years of fighting in making contact with the masses and fighting amid hardships, and to take the road of becoming one with the workers and peasants. They hope that their children will grow up in comfortable circumstances and enjoy life in hothouses. Therefore, when the Party persons in authority taking the capitalist road raised the signboard of "looking after the welfare of the cadres" and started to set up collective boarding schools for the children of cadres so that these students would be entitled to special treatment in politics and living, they came forward quickly and sent their children to these schools.

The persons in the Party in authority taking the capitalist road have intentionally taken advantage of the bourgeois ideology in the minds of the cadres; however, the latter have never expected that behind the signboard of "looking after the welfare of the cadres," there are rolling dark clouds showing a big black flag of a scheme to transform the world!

In foreign countries, the imperialist prophets have, on the basis of changes taking place in the Soviet Union, also pinned their hopes for peaceful evolution on the third and fourth generations of the Party in China, and on such a revisionist educational system as ours, which fosters the privileged strata.

In short, the existence and development of the collective boarding schools for children of the cadres meets the requirements of the bourgeoisie in the country represented by Liu Shao-ch'i and Teng Hsiao-p'ing in carrying out the restoration of capitalism in China, and meets the requirements of the imperialists and revisionists in foreign countries to engineer a "peaceful evolution" in our country.

3

The collective boarding schools for children of cadres have been deeply influenced by the old educational systems and have become a compound of feudalist, bourgeois, and revisionist educational systems.

Through this educational system runs a black line which is a bourgeois educational line represented by Liu Shao-ch'i, Teng Hsiao-p'ing, and Lu Ting-i.

The key idea which this black line of education has spread among the collective boarding schools for children of cadres is special privileges, and more special privileges!

In other words, they are promoting special privileges and benefits, infusing into the students the thought of special privileges, and fostering privileged strata!

Just to promote special privileges and benefits in the work of recruiting students, these schools have openly opposed Chairman Mao's teachings to turn one's face toward the workers and peasants and "to give priority to the workers and peasants and their children in receiving education." They have introduced a strict system of preference so that not only have the children of the broad workers and peasants been refused admission, but the decision whether or not the children of cadres may enter these collective boarding schools for children of cadres is made on the basis of the official ranks of their parents.

Just to foster specially privileged strata these schools have openly opposed and revised Chairman Mao's educational policy by refusing to foster laboring people with socialist consciousness and culture. Instead, they have openly declared themselves for fostering spiritual aristocrats who are sitting tight over the laboring people and "keeping their four limbs idle and making no distinction among the five kinds of grain." They even told the students: "In future you should become generals, ministers, and prime ministers. You are the hardcore of the successors and should not go around selling soy and vinegar."

Just to infuse the thought of special privileges, in the area of political thought these schools have openly opposed Chairman Mao's theory on class and class struggle; instead of promoting the ideological revolutionization of the young people, they have spread the absurd idea of being "born Red," rejected the necessity of ideological reform among the children of the cadres, and infused into them the reactionary feudalist "theory of lineage" by saying that "the children of the cadres are the successors by lineage to our proletarian revolutionary cause."

Just to ensure the birth of privileged strata, schools of this category have, in the field of education, openly opposed letting politics take command, refused to study Chairman Mao's works hard and, instead, given priority to intellectual education, let academic achievements take command, and frantically tried to increase the number of graduates who could pass the entrance examination to higher institutes of education with a view to enabling their students to climb up to the position of privileged strata through the channel of continuously attending schools of a higher grade. In the last ten years and more, only a very few graduates from schools of this category have gone to mountainous and rural areas to undertake common physical labor.

Just to promote special privileges and benefits, in the matter of living conditions these schools have openly opposed Chairman Mao's teachings on guarding against special privileges and running all enterprises with diligence and frugality. They have built gorgeous premises and made living very comfortable and plentiful. They have asked their teachers to act as the "mothers" of the students by busily engaging in looking after the students' personal clothing, food, and lodging. They have told the students to pay attention to their "life" by taking care "not to be drowned when swimming, not to be shot during target practice, not to crash to death when practicing gliding, and not to fall to death while mountain climbing."

From all the above-mentioned facts, we can see that the collective boarding schools for children of cadres are the compound of feudalist, bourgeois, and revisionist educational systems, because of their special privileges, because they are the hotbed for breeding the seeds of revisionism and the tools of Party persons in authority taking the capitalist road represented by Liu Shao-ch'i and Teng Hsiao-p'ing, who are trying hopelessly to restore capitalism in China.

4

The moment has come to thoroughly liquidate and smash into pieces the collective boarding schools for children of cadres.

Chairman Mao has said: "To ensure that our Party and

nation will not change their colors, we not only need our correct lines and policies but also have to foster and train thousands upon thousands of successors to our proletarian revolutionary cause." The collective boarding schools for children of cadres foster only privileged strata and are creating conditions for a "peaceful evolution" toward capitalism. To foster successors to our proletarian revolutionary cause, we must cherish the spirit of "seizing the day, seizing the hour" and topple to the ground this hotbed for breeding the seeds of revisionism! This has a bearing upon the destiny of our Party and our nation, and upon the very important problem of the strategic significance of safeguarding our proletarian state by forever maintaining its colors.

The "16 Points" pointed out: "One of the exceedingly important tasks of the current proletarian Cultural Revolution is to reform the old educational system and reform the old policies and methods of teaching." The revisionist collective boarding schools for children of cadres constitute a stubborn bulwark of the worst crimes under the old educational system. We should take it as an opening for a breakthrough in our general offensive against the whole front of old education, concentrate our firing power, and open fire at the same time! Amid the rumbles of gunfire, the countless crimes of the old educational system will be exposed in the broad daylight! Amid the rumbles of gunfire, the poisons spread by the germs of the old educational system will be thoroughly washed away!

"With power and to spare we must pursue the tottering foe." Smashing into pieces the collective boarding schools for children of cadres is only the beginning of the struggle and not its end. We have to wipe out all the social bases and sources of thinking which generate revisionism by carrying out long-term hard struggles.

Comrades of the revolutionary teachers and students!

The moment for burying the bourgeois educational line represented by Liu Shao-ch'i, Teng Hsiao-p'ing, and Lu Ting-i has come!

Let us give play to our proletarian revolutionary rebel

spirit and throw the hotbed breeding the seeds of revisionism into the garbage bin of history!

Let us dash out from the "paradise of another world," walk with chin up and with big strides onto the road of making an alliance with the workers and peasants, steel ourselves and grow up in the actual struggles of the three great revolutionary movements!

"People are talking about the violent changes in nature." Let us look forward to the future. Our educational position must be a new type, of the great school of Mao Tse-tung's thought, and a good classroom for training successors to our proletarian revolutionary cause.

Amid the clarion songs of triumph, the great red banner of Mao Tse-tung's thought will forever flutter high on the position of education!

The Chingkangshan Fighting Corps of Peking Normal University for Smashing the Collective Boarding Schools for Children of Cadres, and the Liaison Center for Smashing the Collective Boarding Schools for Children of Cadres

THE REBIRTH OF THE WEI-KUO PRIMARY SCHOOL

Prior to the great Cultural Revolution, the Wei-kuo Primary School was a school of the aristocratic type, a revisionist collective boarding school for children of cadres. The persons in authority taking the capitalist road were opposed to Mao Tse-tung's thought, and tried by any and all means to give a very comfortable life to their students. They had made strict restrictions on recruiting new students. As a result, the children of workers and peasants were entirely barred from the school. Even those railway workers and poor and lower-middle peasants who were living right at the doorsteps of the Wei-kuo Primary School had to send their children a distance of several *li* to a general school. Why in these days of socialism do we still find such a system of education? It's because we have the black head-quarters of Liu Shao-ch'i and Teng Hsiao-p'ing. Under the domination of their reactionary line, the wise directive, issued by the State Council in 1955, to gradually abolish special schools for the children of cadres has never been enforced and has been pigeonholed for a long time. They have openly opposed Mao Tse-tung's thought, opposed the educational line of Chairman Mao, and tried hopelessly to drag the schools for children of cadres onto the side-track of revisionism and capitalism!

Our most respected and beloved leader Chairman Mao personally started the fire of the great proletarian Cultural Revolution. In these schools for children of cadres, the revolutionary teachers and students and staff members and personnel have stood up to rebel against the persons in the Party in authority taking the capitalist road, against the revisionist educational system, and have smashed to pieces the old educational system.

The storm of the January revolution has swept across the whole country. The spring of 1967 is a very unusual spring. This spring, the great Cultural Revolution has won a new victory. The Wei-kuo Primary School has gained a new life. It has shown boundless youth and vitality. The reborn Wei-kuo Primary School is a school of Mao Tse-tung's thought. It is a school belonging to the broad masses of workers and peasants. An invigorating new atmosphere is permeating the whole school.

The revolutionary rebels of the Wei-kuo Primary School have rebelled vigorously against the old system and have re-opened classes to make revolution in response to the call of the Party. They have personally paid visits to the poor and lower-middle peasants and registered their names so that they may send their children to the school in the neighborhood. A railway worker said emotionally: "We are grateful to Chairman Mao! We are grateful to him for having started this great Cultural Revolution!" A poor peasant commune member said: "The Wei-kuo Primary School has taken on my child. I could never have believed it even in my dreams in the past!" One parent told his child: "You should thank Chairman Mao, and obey his words! If Chairman Mao did not start this great proletarian Cultural Revolution, you could never step through the door of this school!"

At present, the Wei-kuo Primary School has enrolled more than 200 children of workers and peasants. Children of cadres living in the neighborhood are also attending the school.

When we approached the Wei-kuo Primary School, we could easily hear the clear and vigorous voices of the young students reading aloud passages from *Quotations from Chairman Mao* and singing songs from *Quotations from Chairman Mao*. When we entered the gate of the school, we saw at once a large poster on the wall: "Learn from Comrade Kuo Chia-hung! Pay respects to Comrade Kuo Chia-hung!" Here the revolutionary teachers and students and staff and personnel had posted their enthusiasm for learning from the hero. On the walls were pasted other slogans: "Resolutely crush the adverse current of restoring capitalism from top to bottom." Here the revolutionary teachers and students and staffs and personnel were launching a counteroffensive against the restoration of capitalism, and making a total revolution!

Soon after the school reopened its classes, the students, with the assistance of their revolutionary teachers, set up their own organization of Young Red Guards and immediately plunged into the fight by conducting struggle, criticism, and transformation. The revolutionary teachers, staff, and personnel warmly acclaimed and supported the students in their revolutionary action. The students also paid serious attention to the various different views of the teachers, staff, and personnel, and made careful investigation and study. One of the Young Red Guards said: "We will find out who are true proletarian revolutionaries and whose views correspond with Mao Tse-tung's thought, and then we will support them." In the course of making revolution together, a new revolutionary relationship between the teachers and the students is being built up.

After class, the students always repair their own desks and chairs and never hesitate to do sanitation work in and outside the classrooms. They are living in a collective of labor and fraternity.

Here they are building up a new relationship among the students. Whoever can hold high the red banner of Mao Tse-tung's thought and learn well Chairman Mao's works will receive general support. The children of cadres and the children of workers and peasants learn from each other, and make up their shortcomings by learning from the merits of others. For the first time, the children of cadres realize that the children of workers and peasants have true class sentiments and the fine qualities of diligence and frugality, and wish to learn from them. The children of cadres reflected: "In this school our fellow students are studying Chairman Mao's works very diligently. They study by carrying their class sentiments with them." "Here the students are not proud of the official ranks of their fathers. Whoever is good in political thought gets general support." "Here the students love to labor and always try to work before the others. When they find any chair broken, they repair it on their own initiative. It's not like in the past, when if I found my own chair broken I would use someone else's chair or wait till someone came to repair mine." "Here fellow students put on simple clothes, unlike in the past when I always wanted to have better food and better clothing." This new type of relationship among students helps greatly to eliminate the idea of enjoying special privileges among children of cadres, and they will then become one with the children of workers and peasants.

In short, at the Wei-kuo Primary School the new students have shown the victory of the proletarian educational line, and brought about a new appearance by turning our faces toward the workers, peasants, and soldiers in our educational enterprise. The new students at the Wei-kuo Primary School are the fruits of the great proletarian Cultural Revolution. The school will turn out large numbers of reliable successors to our proletarian revolutionary cause. The new students of the Wei-kuo Primary School are a great victory for Mao Tse-tung's thought. Under the great banner of Mao Tse-tung's thought, a beautiful scene of variegated flowers will surely appear on the educational front.

At the Wei-kuo Primary School, the educational revolution has broken the fetters of the revisionist educational system. It has made only the first step in the 10,000-*li*-long expedition. Hereafter, the road ahead is still very long, and our tasks are more difficult. The revolutionary rebels will continue to forge ahead bravely along the route of navigation opened by Chairman Mao. Though resistance may be very great, we will certainly sail upstream in face of the resistance. The law of history tells us that newly born things will eventually replace rotten things, and a few mantises can never stop the chariot of history with their feelers. Let us win our new victories under the guidance of the great and invincible Mao Tse-tung's thought, and turn the Wei-kuo Primary School into a school of Mao Tse-tung's thought like the Anti-Japanese University in Yenan.

> The Liaison Center for Smashing Thoroughly the System of Collective Boarding Schools for Children of Cadres

PLACE YOUR CHILDREN IN THE BROAD WORLD

Recently, I received in the mail material concerning the great Cultural Revolution and letters to parents from three revolutionary organizations including the "Mao Tse-tung's Thought" Fighting Corps of the Peking Yü-ying Primary School, and these gave me great enlightenment and encouragement.

Smashing the collective boarding schools for children of high-ranking cadres is a revolutionary action. I give it my total approval and unreserved support. These schools are the product of revisionism and are exceedingly harmful. They have many disadvantages but no advantage to us. The students enjoy superior living, receive special treatment, and have long been isolated from the society, from the workers and peasants, and from labor, thus forming a privileged class. They are gradually poisoned and harmed by revisionism. They compete with one another in eating better food, putting on better clothes, showing the better living conditions of their families, and claiming their parents have higher official positions. How can these schools turn out successors to our proletarian revolutionary cause according to Chairman Mao's proposition? Such revisionist schools run entirely counter to Chairman Mao's thoughts on education.

Facts have proved that the students of these schools have long been isolated from the workers and peasants, think intensely about being "born Red," always show their superiority, and will easily be poisoned by revisionism.

During the current great Cultural Revolution, we have seen countless shocking incidents in such schools, and these have effectively demonstrated the crimes of the system of these collective boarding schools for children of cadres. In the course of the movement, not a few students were influenced by the bourgeois reactionary line and poisoned by the lineage theory. They clamored noisily: "My father is a hero, so am I. Your father is a bad egg." They praised highly the reactionary lineage theory and openly spoke against Chairman Mao's revolutionary line. Those whom they acknowledged as members of the "five Red categories" were considered unquestionable revolutionaries. Those who came from undesirable families were categorically rejected. My son so-and-so was seriously poisoned by the influence of this lineage theory. We had to make great efforts before we could change him and before he began to come over to the side of Chairman Mao's revolutionary line and rebel against the bourgeois reactionary line.

In the course of the movement, some children of high cadres beat people and cursed them, destroyed public property, and squandered freely the wealth of the state. Others held fast to a reactionary stand, put up reactionary posters, and maintained persistent resistance against their revolutionary teachers. How could we help but feel sorry for them? If these schools should remain one more day, they would do another day's harm to our revolutionary next generation, that is, it would constitute a crime against the people. We must place our children in the society and among the masses of the workers and peasants so that they will gradually understand the thoughts and sentiments of the working people and become laborers with socialist consciousness and culture. We should assume our responsibilities toward the revolution, toward the people, and toward our revolutionary next generation to ensure that our state will not be revisionist and will never change its color. We have to make our offspring for thousands of generations be loyal forever to the Party and to Chairman Mao. We have to rebel thoroughly against this old educational system.

Chairman Mao has said: "Everything reactionary is the same; if you don't hit it, it won't fall." We should apply the spirit of "seizing the day and seizing the hour" to smash to pieces this product of revisionism—the collective boarding schools for children of high cadres! Hell to all these things in contravention of Mao Tse-tung's thought!

While we rebel against the bourgeois reactionary line and against the revisionist educational system, we must also rebel against "selfishness" in our heads and cultivate devotion to "public interests"; that is, we must take ourselves as a moving force of the revolution and also as a target of the revolution. We must resolutely oppose all bourgeois thoughts of only looking after one's private interests and paying no attention to collective interests, and oppose all speeches and actions undermining the great Cultural Revolution. We should see that since the great Cultural Revolution is a revolution, it is bound to meet with resistance. Such resistance may come from persons in authority taking the capitalist road, from the force of habit of the old society, or from narrow-minded and muddle-headed people. You must have heard some people say: "You should take into consideration my difficulties!" "I give support to your revolutionary action. But I must let my children stay in the school for another one or two years!" Some others even openly raised objections: "If you fail to arrange boarding and lodging for my boy, I won't send him to another school next year or the year after next. . . ." That's quite enough. Those who had such views could not give up the old revisionist things and wished that their children could continue to enjoy special privileges in isolation from the society, from workers and peasants, and from labor, thus doing harm to our revolutionary next generation. Should we fail to get rid of the styles of the old officials and old squires and eliminate bourgeois thinking, failing to burn out the "selfishness" in our heads during the great Cultural Revolution movement, we will lift a rock just to drop it on our own feet and take our own medicine!

I believe that whether or not one gives support to the revolutionary action of the rebels is a matter of one's stand. Whether or not the old educational system should be smashed into pieces depends on whether we are going to bring up our next generation for socialist revolution or whether we wish to bring up a revisionist next generation. It is an important political problem which is related to the existence or extinction of our state. All revolutionary cadres and revolutionary comrades have our definite responsibilities and should work together to carry out our historical revolutionary mission of smashing the old educational system! "There is no construction without destruction, and there is no flowing without blocking." Only by completely smashing the revisionist educational system can we turn it into a great red school of Mao Tse-tung's thought.

Comrade revolutionary rebels! We will resolutely cooperate with you, fight shoulder to shoulder with you, break through all the obstacles and strive together in criticizing the bourgeois reactionary line and smashing the revisionist educational system! We swear to carry the great proletarian Cultural Revolution through to the end and win our complete victory! Let us shout aloud:

"Long live the great Communist Party of China!"

"A long life, and a long long life to the reddest red sun in our hearts, Chairman Mao!"

Ch'eng Chien-ying,
parent of a student